MW01042414

Cheap Thrills Montreal

Cheap Thrills
MONTREAL

Great Montreal Meals
for under $15.00

[2003]

Nancy Marrelli
& Simon Dardick

Véhicule Press

Véhicule Press acknowledges the support of the Government of Canada's Book Industry Development Program

Cover illustration: Bruce Roberts
Cover art direction and design: JW Stewart
Special thanks to Vicki Marcok, and Matt Huculak
Inside imaging: Simon Garamond
Printing: AGMV-Marquis Inc.

CATALOGUING IN PUBLICATION DATA

Nancy Marrelli & Simon Dardick
Cheap thrills Toronto : great Montreal meals
for under $15

ISBN 1-55065-165-X

1. Restaurants–Quebec–Montreal–Guidebooks.
I. Marrelli, Nancy. II. Dardick, Simon, 1943-

TX907.5 C22 T67 2001   647.95713'541

Published by Véhicule Press
P.O.B. 125, Place du Parc Station
Montréal, Québec H2X 4A3

514.844.6073   FAX 514.844.7543

www.vehiculepress.com
www.cheapthrillsguides.com

CANADIAN DISTRIBUTION
LPG Distribution Collective
800-591-6250

U.S. DISTRIBUTION
Independent Publishers Group, Chicago, Illinois
800-888-4741

Printed in Canada

Contents

What is a Cheap Thrill?

The restaurants in this book generally offer meals at dinner for $15 or less. This does not mean that every meal in the restaurant will be under $15, but there should be a reasonable selection in that price range before taxes, tip, and alcohol.

☙

Independent Reviews

We pride ourselves on the independence of our reviews. No offers of free food or any other gratuities are ever accepted by our reviewers.

☙

Check It Out Before You Go

Restaurants change constantly—menus, hours, and owners are in constant flux. The information in this book was current at the time of publication, but there's no guarantee that things won't change without warning. It's a good idea to call ahead.

This book would not be possible without our reviewers and contributors...

Phyllis Aronoff
Byron Ayanoglu
Emily Beauregard
John Beauregard
Gerry Bergeron
John Bergeron
Howard Bokser
David Bourgeois
Ann Charney
Mel Charney
Denys Chouinard
Anne Dardick
Rosemary Dardick
Jacqueline Davis
Hugh Doisin
Mathilde Doisin
Suzanne Duranceau
David Engle
Louise Fabiani
Arden Ford
Carlos Fraenkel
Kim Fraser
Marie Gauthier
Katherine Gombay
Anne Greengrove-Beauregard
Sarah Haggard
Bruce Henry
Vicki Percival Hilton
Nathalie Hodgson
Lindsay Holmgren
Matthew Huculak
Alan Hustak
Jon Kalina
Martine Klubal

Barry Lazar
David Leblanc
Mathieu Lemay
Jennifer-Clare Little
Oisin Little
Denis Longchamps
Karel-Martin Ludvik
John MacCallum
Sara Magrin
Vicki Marcok
Maria Marrelli
Joan McSheffrey
Savin Mhaiki
Lisa Morris
Øystein Nordengen
Leslie Orr
Vincent Ouellette
Colin Pearson
Sandra Phillips
Shelley Pomerance
Stan Posner
Tom Puchniak
George Rice
Nicholas Robinson
Margaret Rumscheidt-Ludvik
Tommy Schnurmacher
Howard Scott
Caroline Sigouin
John Stewart
Lucina Tar Haar
Karen Teoh
Louis Toner
Brian Van den Broek
Carole Welp
Janis Zubalik
Chantal Zumbrunn

Introduction

Montreal is an incredible food city! It's a place where people eat well and thoroughly enjoy the sociability of eating out. You can eat your way through many cultures and cuisines, and you can do it to fit almost any pocketbook

This book is about eating well in Montreal. It is an adventure into many parts of a fascinating city in search of good food at reasonable prices. *Cheap Thrills Montreal* includes our own homegrown specialties as well as culinary traditions from the rainbow mix of people who live here. The roots of Montrealers run long and deep and our collective past is vibrantly reflected in the food we eat.

Montrealers love to eat out. We eat out for many reasons: we're too busy or frazzled to cook every day, we travel, or we prefer to share food with friends or family without doing the cooking! We look for affordable pleasure and for adventure. This is the fourth edition of a book that set out to discover Montrealers' favourite inexpensive restaurants. The list of reviewers and contributors is in the front of the book: we thank them all for their good appetite, judgement, and willingness to share their discoveries with us.

A "cheap thrill" is $15 or less for dinner, before taxes, tip, and alcohol. Many of our selections are well below the limit and a few are hugging the top. We have raised the limit from $10 to $15 for the first time since 1996 to keep pace with rising costs and to ensure that a wide selection is available to our readers. Of course the food has to be excellent, not just cheap!

Cheap Thrills is a celebration of the wonderful food available in Montreal, and the diverse cultures that have been interwoven into the fabric of this beautiful city that is a young 360 years old. We are fortunate to share this diversity whether our ancestors arrived here with Jeanne Mance in 1642, we recently emigrated, or are just visiting. *Cheap Thrills Montreal* will take you around the city and around the world.

This is how Montreal eats!

Alphabetical Listing of Restaurants

L'Abidjanaise

5772 Decelles (at Côte-Ste-Catherine)
Métro: Côte-des-Neiges
Phone: 514.223.1147
Hours: 5pm-11pm daily
Credit cards: cash only; Alcohol: all
Wheelchair access: entrance yes; restroom yes
Average main course: $10

L'Abidjanaise serves West African/Ivory Coast food in Côte-des-Neiges.

L'Abidjanaise cooks traditional Ivory Coast food with its deep West African roots, and does it very well indeed. The basic starches are plantain, yams, manioc, rice, and corn. Ground nuts/peanuts are a staple and New World foods like okra, plantains, chillies, and coconuts are integrated into the cooking. They were brought back to Africa (and Europe) in returning ships during the slave trade. Portions are extremely generous, and house-made hot sauce with a powerful kick is available on request. Choose savoury West African standards like chicken yassa with lemons and onions, thieboudiene (baked fish with spices), gumbo, and the Ivorian national dish kedjenou, chicken with onions and tomato in delicious sauce. Don't miss the beef mafé—beef, garlic, onions, and chillies in a generous quantity of rich and unctuous peanut sauce that is good to the last drop! Homemade sorbets are a perfect ending if you have room.

The restaurant is in a small nondescript commercial strip in a residential area but the space is long and large with tables for large groups and some African art on the walls. Three Montrealers from West Africa (Lance, Lidge, and Marcelin) opened L'Abidjanaise in 2001, and it is slowly evolving. They will soon add a table d'hôte menu and live music, as well as new dishes garnered from family and friends. Ivory Coast has 16 million people, 60 ethnic groups, and 77 living languages; it shares many foods with its West African neighbours. Keep tuned to see what new dishes show up at L'Abidjanaise—an inexpensive and delicious ticket to an interesting corner of West Africa.

L'Académie

4051 St. Denis (at Duluth)
Métro: Sherbrooke or Mont-Royal
Phone: 514.849.2249
Hours: 11am-10:30pm daily
Credit cards: V, MC, Amex, Interac; Alcohol: BYOB
Wheelchair access: no
Average pasta: $9.50; mussels: $10

L'Académie on St-Denis is hugely popular for Italian and French bistro-style food on a budget.

Pastas are a good deal, with very generous and savoury portions. Veal dishes include the Italian standards, tender and delicate. Seafood dishes are outside the *Cheap Thrills* guidelines as are steaks, and much of the table d'hôte menu, but portions are so large that two can eat heartily with one appetizer and one main dish or table d'hôte selection. For appetizers, artichoke salad with light vinaigrette on a bed of mixed greens is outstanding, and their coquille St-Jacques is a fresh and creamy version. Main course sole meunière is a winner with a light sauce that complements but doesn't drown the fish. Cannelloni al forno is a popular choice. Mussels come in nine varieties (Roquefort, vodka/tomato, pesto…), and are served with house-made fries. The menu doesn't leap towards new territory but they produce reliably good standards to feed you well without breaking the bank.

The St-Denis digs replace the original that opened in 1984 and burned down in 1999. The chef has been there since the beginning. There are three floors with comfortable chairs, and it's all airy and agreeable, with attentive and accommodating staff who do not rush you. This is a fun place for groups. There's often a crowd at the door between 7 and 9 p.m. and reservations are possible only Monday through Wednesday, and at off-peak hours the rest of the week. You will never be unpleasantly surprised at L'Académie.

Agostini

5545 Upper Lachine Rd. (near Girouard)
Métro: Vendôme, then 90 or 104 bus
Phone: 514.485.0235
Hours: Mon-Sat 11am-9pm; closed Sunday
Credit cards: cash only; Alcohol: all
Wheelchair access: entrance yes; restroom yes
Daily Special table d'hôte: $8.50-$9.95 (prices include tax)

Agostini is a home-style Italian restaurant with wonderful Italian subs.

Specials of the day include homemade soup, a choice from three main courses such as lasagne, roast pork or chicken, salmon steak, linguini with clams, and coffee. It's one of the best buys in town! The menu also includes à la carte pasta and veal specialties, pizza, and Italian submarine sandwiches. You could become addicted to their sausage sub: a crusty bun brimming with browned split sausage, smothered with onions fried to melting perfection, tomato, and coleslaw or lettuce—it's a messy delight. You can pig out with the 14-inch but the half (7-inch) with optional double sausage is enough for most people. "Some like it hot" and if you do be sure to opt for a topping of the tasty, zingy hot pepper sauce—a house specialty so popular they now sell containers to take out! Fresh fruit is a good dessert choice. Smooth espresso and cappuccino are excellent. They do take-out and deliver in the neighbourhood. All prices include taxes. It's tried and true rather than adventurous but the food is unfailingly good. They do special meals for Christmas Eve and Valentine's Day.

Agostini is pleasant and bright but not plush. Children are welcome and service is friendly and efficient, although it's hectic at lunch. This is the kind of good food an Italian mom might make. Maria and Ezio Agostini arrived from Italy in the late 1950s and they run the restaurant with their children Mario and Antoinetta. There's enough homemade good food to be able to eat here almost every day—and some locals do just that!

Au Bec Fin JRR

5607 Ave. du Parc (bet. St-Viateur & Bernard)
Bus: 80 (du Parc), 535 at rush our
Phone: 514.278.6134
Hours: noon-8pm daily; closed Sunday
Credit cards: cash only; Alcohol: no
Wheelchair accessible: entrance yes; restroom yes
Average main course: *$10*

Au Bec Fin serves Haitian "cuisine de maman" on Avenue du Parc.

Haitian Créole cooking is a seamless blend of African, French, and traditional Haitian influences. It uses lots of lime juice, sour orange, hot peppers, and staples such as plantain, cassava, rice, and fresh fruit. The neatly written daily menu is on the chalkboard behind the counter where you order your food. Find yourself a seat amidst the Haitian taxi drivers here for authentic Haitian comfort food and wait for a "maman" to bring you steaming plates on a plain brown tray. Almost everything comes with plantain, fresh crisp salad, and rice and beans in various incarnations—perfect accompaniments. Griot (or grillot) is the national dish and it's not to be missed. Chunks of moist, tender, and tasty fried pork with a slightly piquant dipping sauce are to die for. A whole red snapper is moist and succulent, steamed over a rich broth of onion and red peppers. Vegetable specials are greens cooked with whatever good happens to be going in the kitchen (not necessarily vegetarian). Cabrit is delicious grilled goat, again with a wonderful dipping sauce. Be adventurous! Try it all! You can even just point to whatever looks good to you. Tropical fruit drinks are interesting and fun. Portions are generous.

Raymonde Brunache came to Montreal from Haiti 30 years ago and she opened Au Bec Fin in 1992. The space is long and narrow, with no fancy décor—this place is about the food. The exterior is unobtrusive and you could very easily walk by without even noticing it's there. This is homey, unpretentious Créole cooking—yum!

B & M

5950 Monkland (corner Royal)
Métro: Villa Maria, then 103 or 162 bus
Phone: 514.484.3717
Hours: Mon-Fri 7am-2am; Sat & Sun 9am-2am
Credit cards: V, MC, Amex; Alcohol: all
Wheelchair access: entrance yes; restroom yes
Average main course: $10

B&M is a Monkland Village hot spot with a vast menu, large portions, and good food.

This menu has almost too many choices, it's a challenge to choose from rotisserie chicken, brochettes, steaks, seafood, Chinese dishes, pizza, pasta, salads, sandwiches, and who knows what all! They manage to pull it all off because everything is fresh and made to order. Pizzas are particularly popular, with a thick crust and myriad toppings in many combinations and sizes. Pastas include cannelloni, spaghetti, linguini, and fettuccine with standard sauces and cheesy "au gratin" versions. Chicken, beef, vegetarian, fish, or combo brochettes are tasty. Salads are large and fresh, with olive oil dressings. There are plenty of vegetarian options. Daily blackboard specials ($8.25-$20) include soup and coffee. Roast beef is on most days and it's a real winner although a little over the *Cheap Thrills* limit at $17 for 12 ounces. The usual breakfast/brunch specialties are reasonably priced. Portions are supergenerous and most people never make it to dessert.

B & M stands for Bob and Mike, the original owners. It was bought in 1983 by Jimmy and Anastasia Farazis, and Kathy, Jimmy, and Chris Soulingis. They turned a greasy spoon into a beloved NDG landmark, popular with all generations, families, and students, and welcoming to people just passing through. Some eat here every day without ever getting bored. It can get busy on weekends but there's always a cheerful good feeling about the place. B & M works because there's lots of variety, portions are big, food is fresh and reliably good, and it's a pleasant, if sometimes crowded, space.

Bangkok

1616 Ste-Catherine W. (Le Faubourg at Guy, 3rd floor)
Métro: Guy-Concordia
Phone: 514.935.2178
Hours: 11am-8:50pm daily
Credit cards: cash only; Alcohol: no
Wheelchair access: entrance yes; restroom yes
Average main course: $6

Yes, you can find really fine Thai food at affordable prices in a downtown food mall!

Bangkok, in Le Faubourg, has exceptionally good Thai food. The chicken soup is outstanding, with real chunks of chicken (coconut milk is optional) and the tart bite of lemongrass. The taste is pure and clear—arguably the best chicken soup in town and a light meal in itself. Set specials are under $7 and include soup or crispy house-made spring rolls and choices like chicken with yellow curry (particularly yummy), cashews or chilli paste, ginger beef, or heavenly BBQ duck with coconut milk. A la carte dishes like pad Thai, garlic and pepper, peanut sauce, and eggplant are available with chicken, beef, seafood or vegetarian options. No pork is served. Eggplant with chicken is sublime, perfumed with fresh basil. Traditional pad Thai is superb in any variation, but the chicken or duck are favourites. Surprise specials are also available. Choose your preferred level of spice or none at all.

Food is made to order (except curries) so everything is fresh with all the complex flavours and textures of Thai cuisine. Chef-owner Somphop Vichenker came here in the 1980s from Bangkok where she had a food stand. She rarely leaves the burners where she creates her special magic, and every dish meets her demanding standards. Husband Santisuk and daughter Patty handle the front with grace and courtesy. The Faubourg can be noisy and crowded at lunch but it's pleasant in the evening and the food is just as good! Bangkok is not to be missed—it's almost too good to be true!

Bar-B Barn

1201 Guy (bet. Ste-Catherine & René Lévesque)
Métro: Guy-Concordia
Phone: 514.931.3811
Hours: Mon-Thurs 11am-10pm; Fri until 11pm;
    Sat 11:30am-midnight; Sun 11:30am-10pm
Credit cards: V, MC, Amex, Interac; Alcohol: all
Wheelchair access: no
Average main course: $11

The Bar-B Barn is a Montreal institution serving terrific ribs—and chicken too.

This is not the place to bring your vegetarian cousin—the menu is broiled ribs, chicken and fixings. The real draw is modest to gluttonous portions of ribs. A chicken/ribs combo is also popular. Most plates are served with a good bun, mashed potatoes or fries (fries are frozen not fresh), and a small salad with commercial dressing. It all seems to work. The ribs are really delicious—long, tender, juicy, and quite lean. They get a slightly sweet final basting, but are not covered in a sticky mess. Gas broiling is long and low-temperature so the meat doesn't dry out or become charred. Have a modest portion of three ribs or go for the "whole hawg" (it's trademarked!) of nine long ones! You can also trade portions back and forth. The chicken is good if you're not into spare ribs, and the chicken on a bun is an inexpensive and delicious option. They have apple pie and cakes if you haven't completely overdosed. There are good lunch deals and kids' specials.

The atmosphere is relaxed and rustic. There are booths, lots of dark wood in several spaces over two floors, a wall of business cards, and signed sports photos. They cater parties upstairs. Owner Manny Barnoff opened Bar-B on Guy Street in 1966, and in Pointe Claire in 1981, and it hasn't really changed much. Tom McQueen is the long-time manager. If you want ribs this is still the place to come!

Batory Euro-Deli

115 St-Viateur W. (near St-Urbain)
Bus: 55 (St-Laurent) or 80 (du Parc)
Phone: 514.948.2161
Hours: Tue 10am-6pm; until 7pm Wed; until 9pm Thurs & Fri;
  Sat 10am-4pm; Sun 9am-2pm; closed Monday
Credit cards: Interac; Alcohol: no
Wheelchair access: no
Average main course: $5

This tiny Polish deli offers wonderful, substantial Polish specialties for eat-in or take-out.

The delectable borsht (two versions, a thicker and a clearer one) makes an excellent starter for the house masterpiece, Polski Talerz, a combination platter *for two*—or one *very* hungry person. This signature meal includes cabbage rolls, pierogies, sauerkraut and sausages. Thick and hearty pea soup sticks to your ribs with chunks of sausage and a great smoky taste. Sausages and sauerkraut counterpoint smoky and sharp tastes. Pierogies (potato, cheese and mushroom) are heads above what you get elsewhere. Cherry and poppy seed cheesecakes are house specialties. The menu and eat-in space are limited but they serve satisfying and delicious home-cooked comfort food. Although vegetarian meals are not really on the radar screen, they do have excellent non-meat pierogies and blintzes. They do a booming take-out business.

Owner Jadwiga Czerkawska and her husband Marek Witkowski opened Batory in 1990. He had previously been a chef on Polish cruise ships, but they both cook at Batory. This is a deli rather than a true restaurant, and there are only five comfortable tables, but there never seems to be a problem. Take-out is their real business, and most dishes are also available frozen. Batory also sells Polish packaged foods, and they even rent Polish movies! It's packed after church on Sundays with parishioners of St. Michael's Church next door. Batory is also a favourite with the locals who appreciate its warm service and delicious and generous home cooking. This is food that makes you feel good.

La Belle Italienne / La Bella Italiana

5884 Jean-Talon Est, St-Léonard (at Lacordaire)

Métro: Cadillac, then 32 bus north

Phone: 514.254.4811

Resto hours: Mon-Fri noon-3pm & 5pm-10pm; Sat 5pm-10pm; closed Sunday.

Café hours: Mon-Thurs 8am-12am; Fri until 2am; Sat 9am-2am; Sun 9am-12am

Credit cards: V, MC, Interac; Alcohol: all

Wheelchair access: entrance yes; restroom yes

Average meal: $12

La Bella Italiana is a relaxed St-Léonard coffee-bar/resto.

They use quality ingredients treating them with respect so anything you order will satisfy. Soup, appetizers, pasta, and sandwiches are ideal budget choices. Soups are a light meal. Chicken soup is chock full of chicken and flavour, perfect with grated cheese, Italian style. A choice of appetizers is a great grazing option. Daily specials are on a chalkboard—the inspiration of the day. Fine Italian pastas are lightly dressed with flavourful sauces or topped with cheese and done *al forno*. Specials like rabbit in white wine, and the veal dishes are out of the *Cheap Thrills* range but this is a perfect spot to blow the budget—quality food and terrific value. A scrumptious selection of ice cream is available. Then there's the coffee! They do all the right things to Moka d'Oro Italian coffee to produce a smooth, full-flavoured cup of pure pleasure.

Bella Italiana started as a gelateria/coffee bar in 1983, but the ice cream hived off long ago. Kathy Gentile bought it in 2000 after working here for 10 years. Mother Rosie cooks during the day and brother Roberto cooks in the evening and these folks from Molise know their stuff. They have a bar licence at the moment so no kids, but this will change soon. There are two rooms, but at night the real scene is around the coffee machines. The kitchen closes around 10 but you can get something light any time. There's a small terrace. It's a friendly place, a neighbourhood hangout for people of all ages. They come for the food, ice cream, superb coffee, and especially for the warm and friendly ambiance. Good food, good coffee, good vibes!

Les Belles Soeurs

2251 Marie-Anne (at Messier)
Métro: Mont-Royal, then 97 bus east
Phone: 514.526.1574
Hours: Mon-Fri 7:30am-10pm; Sat & Sun 9am-10pm
Credit cards: V, MC, Interac; Alcohol: beer & wine
Wheelchair access: entrance yes; restroom no
Average main course: $9

This charming and unpretentious neighbourhood resto serves tasty food with a healthy twist.

The menu at Les Belles Soeurs is put together with care and attention to health concerns, cost considerations, and the quality of the food. The house specialties include Hamburger Belles Soeurs, a juicy lamb patty with mushrooms, feta, emmental, spinach, and mayo, all on a fresh challah bun with sesame seeds. Vegetarians will appreciate the veggie hot dog. The fries are fresh cut and cooked in peanut oil so they're worth the indulgence. Mussels come with all-you-can-eat fries and on Monday to Wednesday evenings they come with a free beer. They have specials every day and they usually include soup and a beverage. Specials are typically pasta or a special plate like veal cutlet. The cheeseburger special includes fries and a small beer. They even have Montignac choices if that's your particular passion. Pasta Belles Soeurs is served in a delicious light tomato sauce with black olives, spinach, and artichoke hearts. Salads are made generously with fresh ingredients. Homemade desserts include crème caramel, sugar pie, and apple pie—be sure to ask to have the apple pie warmed. They have an extensive breakfast menu and the weekend brunch specials are worth going out of your way for.

Les Belles Soeurs is a friendly place with fun, quirky decorations, and lighthearted attitude. Annie Houle and Denise Larocque (both from Drummondville) opened here in 1995 and with tongue-in-cheek they describe their food as chic snacks, Drummondville-style.

La Binerie Mont-Royal

367 Mont-Royal E. (at St-Denis)
Métro: Mont-Royal
Phone: 514.285.9078
Hours: Mon-Fri 6am-8pm; Sat & Sun 7:30am-3pm
Credit cards: cash only; Alcohol: no
Wheelchair access: no
Daily specials: *$5.99*

La Binerie is in a time warp: it's a 1940s working-class diner on the Plateau Mont-Royal.

The day starts with breakfast of various combinations of eggs, bacon, sausage, toast, cretons, and baked beans. The house specialty is baked beans and bread, with optional sausages. A complete three-course lunch or dinner includes pea soup, dessert and beverage. Choices include diner specialties like macaroni with meat, beef with cabbage, sausages, shepherd's pie, and Québécois specialties like tourtière, ragoût de boulettes, and cretons. The House Special ("Assiette Maison") is a combo of tourtière, ragoût de boulettes, and baked beans—all the specialties of the house rolled into one extravaganza—and at $8.95 this is the most expensive item on the menu. Dessert is the Binerie's famous pudding chômeur. Everything is made on the premises from closely guarded recipes. It's impossible to leave here hungry!

There are absolutely no frills in this small friendly place— a family-run business with only 11 stools and 4 tables. Started in 1940, it has stayed in the family and everything is very much like it has always been. La Binerie serves the kind of food that makes you feel you should go out and chop down some trees after eating!

Bistro Gourmet 2

4007 St-Denis (cor. Duluth)
Métro: Sherbrooke or Mont-Royal
Phone: 514.844.0555
Hours: Mon-Fri 11:30am-3pm; Mon-Sun 6-10pm; Sun brunch
11am-3pm
Credit cards: V, MC, Interac; Alcohol: yes
Wheelchair access: yes
Daily specials: *$15.00 at night, $9.95 at lunch*

Bistro Gourmet II is a quintessential French bistro on St-Denis.

The menu is quite straightforward. There are eight classic bistro meals available for a fixed price of $14.99, including soup or salad. Dessert and beverage are not included so it's doesn't quite fit the *Cheap Thrills* framework at dinner, but it's close and such a great deal that we've included it anyway. Indulge a little and have their excellent coffee and dessert. The same dishes and some others are available with dessert and coffee at slightly higher prices. Currently the choices are: grilled bavette with Dijon mustard, trout with Auvergne blue cheese, lamb shank with rosemary, veal kidneys with Calvados, roulade of sole with white wine, supreme of chicken with green peppercorns, and mussels. The lamb shanks and calves liver are particularly good choices but everything is well prepared bistro style. Portions are generous and presentation is done with flair and high style.

This is an offshoot of the original Bistro Gourmet downtown, an established tiny but excellent bistro. They are both owned by Gabriel Ohana and his daughter Nathalie. The branch had some early growing pains but things have settled down and the food is exactly what you would expect from a good bistro in Paris. Service is very professional and polished. There is a lovely outdoor terrace and the interior is simple, elegant and uncluttered. This is a perfect choice for a special night out or for a lovely meal with your visiting great aunt.

Bombay Mahal

1001 Jean-Talon W. (at Birnam)
Métro: L'Acadie
Phone: 514.273.3331
Hours: Tue-Sat 11am-10:30pm; Sun 11am-9pm; closed Monday
Credit cards: cash only; Alcohol: no
Wheelchair access: no
Average main course: $6

Bombay Mahal on Jean-Talon West serves outstanding Gujarati-style food.

There are two quite separate streams of food here: many strictly vegetarian dishes and a good selection of meat dishes. Cooking is Gujarat style but there are some South Indian specialties as well. They make sublime masala dosa, and they do it the long way, making their own batter of fermented rice and dal (lentils). The dosas are long, toasty, thin, and lacy handfuls, rolled around a delicious filling and served with sambal and chutney—a truly impressive house specialty. They make their own paneer and spinach paneer is a favourite. Tandoor choices include chicken, goat, and shrimp, or a combo dish. Tandoor chicken leg (drumstick and thigh) with salad has to be one of the best buys in town at $1.99! Black lentils with spices are a special treat. Chicken, lamb, and goat dishes are filled with flavour and spicy goodness! Thalis are always a good way to taste a variety of things and they're available until 9 p.m. Onion badji is outstanding with a tamarind sauce, and excellent nan and roti are fresh from the tandoor oven. They used to sell sweets but only gulab jam is available now. Take-out and catering is a large part of their business.

Bombay Mahal ("mahal" means "palace") opened in 1998. The original owner was from Bombay but in 2001 it was sold to Ruksmani Bhandari. Cook and manager Prashant Daroo-wala, originally a lawyer in Gujarat, came to Canada in 1991 and he has been here since the beginning, maintaining consistent quality and style. Weekends can be busy. Don't expect anything fancy—this is non-décor. But the food is excellent and prices are rock bottom!

La Cabane

3872 St-Laurent (at Napoléon)
Bus: 55 (St-Laurent)
Phone: 514.843.7283
Hours: 11:30am-3am daily
Credit cards: V, MC, Amex, Interac; Alcohol: all
Wheelchair access: entrance yes; restroom yes
Daily specials: $7-$12

La Cabane is a resto-bar serving good food at all hours in a convivial spot on St-Laurent Boulevard.

The chalkboards give the daily specials (including veggies, fries/rice, coffee) and they usually include a pasta dish, fresh fish (e.g., salmon steak), a game dish, and a combo plate such as lamb chops/quail/sausage. They're a good deal. Many dishes are charcoal grilled to perfection in the Portuguese style. Brochettes are popular and the fries are superb—fresh potatoes cooked properly in vegetable shortening! Light and crusty Portuguese rolls are excellent and they make wonderful sandwiches (grilled pork is a favourite). Portions are generous. Petisco is a hefty appetizer or main meal of grilled pork and sausages with cheese—wonderfully addictive! The 14-ounce rib steak is a $15 glutton feast! Meat and fish lovers will be very happy here but vegetarians will find comfort with the Greek salad. Draft beer in pitchers (including local microbrews) is the accompaniment of choice. If you can manage dessert, treat yourself to a glass of fine port or, in season, pop next door for a Ripples ice cream.

It's friendly, casual, and comfortable with a youngish crowd. Front windows open up in good weather. The kitchen closes at 2:30 a.m. so it's a great place to go for a late meal. Abilio Carrera bought La Cabane in 1980 and, since his death in 2000, sons Martin, Amerigo, and Eugenio have kept it much the same as it has always been. La Cabane is a good place to while away a pleasant afternoon or evening with a satisfying meal and a pleasant drink, or some of both.

Café Brazil

5390 Ave. du Parc (at St-Viateur)
Bus: 80 (du Parc)
Phone: 514.270.7001
Hours: 10am-8pm daily
Credit cards: cash only; Alcohol: no
Wheelchair access: entrance yes; restroom no
Average main course: $6

Café Brazil serves delicious fresh juices and Brazilian specialties on Avenue du Parc.

The set menu is modest but in addition to various small snack foods, there are daily specials that are excellent value. A large soup of the day is a small meal, fresh, homemade, and chock full of good things! You can get things like hamburgers but it's best to go Brazilian all the way! Pork and chicken are simply prepared, deep fried without batter, and crispy, but somehow not dried out. Sides are rice and beans and a fresh salad with plain but good vinaigrette. Fabulous feijoada, Brazil's signature national dish, is available on Saturday and Sunday, a wonderful mixture of special meats and black beans, served with fresh greens, rice and other goodies! Fiery hot sauce is served on the side, Brazilian-style. It's a special treat and a great deal at $12. They often run out so reserve it earlier in the week. Fresh fruit drinks are terrific by themselves or as wonderful accompaniment to the food.

Café Brazil is very small, cheerfully homey, comfortably relaxed, and decidedly friendly. It opened in May 2002 and Brazilian owner Ana Maria Perreira also does catering. The café is a family affair and partner Luis Betancourt (a Cuban singer) is also involved. They will expand the menu as they become better established. This is a sunny little place that will cheer you up summer or winter with simple good food and drink and a friendly welcome.

Café L'Étranger

680 Ste-Catherine W. (near Université)
Métro: McGill
Phone: 514.392.9016
Hours: Mon-Wed 9am-11pm; until 12am Thurs & Fri; Sat 10am-12am; Sun 11am-11pm
Credit cards: V, MC, Interac; Alcohol: all
Wheelchair access: no
Specials of the Day: $8-$10

Café L'Étranger serves a wide selection of comfort food in a relaxed spot, a few steps down, in the heart of Downtown.

The sheer abundance of the menu is overwhelming: salads, snacks, sandwiches, burgers, pizza, panini, and wraps. The daily menu (11a.m.-11p.m.) changes weekly and it includes breakfast, a burger, panini, Caesar salad, a pasta, and a few substantial dishes like chicken pot pie or sweet and sour meatballs. Snack/appetizers Hunan dumplings (great sauce), and stuffed jalapenos are dynamite. Salads are fresh and tossed with a variety of good dressings. The menu has 13 varieties of grilled cheese sandwich—a staggering but deliciously interesting array, served with the signature crunchy pasta chips. Sandwiches and burgers come in interesting combinations with grilled veggies and other goodies. Ice cream desserts are huge extravaganzas that could be shared by a group. The candy bar fiesta is utterly decadent! The bar serves novelty mixed drinks and a large selection of imported beer and local microbrews.

Doreen Tang and Rick Mok opened L'Étranger in 1998, the name inspired by the Camus novel, and it aims to be a place where strangers can feel at home, have a drink or a meal, or settle in to read something from the bookshelves. Kitchen and wait staff are young, energetic, and they keep things moving. It's a good place to go for lunch, dinner, or a snack while shopping, after a movie or a hard day at the office. This is a pleasant downtown place with good food and reasonable prices.

Café International

6714 St-Laurent Blvd. (near St-Zotique)
Métro: Beaubien, or 55 bus (St-Laurent)
Phone: 514.495.0067
Hours: 8am-3am daily
Credit Cards: V, MC, Interac; Alcohol: all
Wheelchair access: entrance (one step); restroom no
Average daily special: $14

This authentic café in Little Italy serves great food, excellent coffee and just the right atmosphere!

Bocconcini and tomato, and calamari fritti appetizers are terrific for grazing. Panini include tuna, chicken, prosciutto, and grilled house sausage. Pizzas are justly popular. Daily specials are new and include pastas, meat, fish, and always a risotto. The kitchen prepares gnocchi on Thursday and tagliatelle on Friday. Food is fresh and good. Coffee is the specialty of the house and it's freshly ground and expertly prepared using an extraordinarily fine house blend, or the divine Illy for decaf. After 10 p.m. you can have only sandwiches or pizza.

Café International (opened 1968) was bought in 2001 by Edmondo Arcaro. Son Marco (Cordon Bleu-Ottawa) is the chef and son Michael is the manager. Food is now front and centre, not an afterthought. There is a long counter where people stand for a quick coffee, European style, but tables and chairs are available for eating and idling. Front windows slide open in summer. A big TV screen documents the sports scene for those interested. You could spend the whole day here, beginning with coffee and a newspaper in the morning, later meeting with family, friends, or lovers. Young and old, strangers and regulars, all feel comfortable here, enjoying the atmosphere, wonderful food, and the fabulous coffee. One of the great pleasures of a Montreal summer evening is sitting at crowded outside tables late into the night, eating, sipping, viewing, and being part of the vibrant passing street scene of Little Italy. Café International is a convivial Italian-style café!

Café Malibran

808 Berri (Old Montreal; at St-Antoine)
Métro: Champs de Mars
Phone: 514.904.2646
Hours: Mon-Sat 8am-7pm; closed Sunday
Credit cards: Interac; Alcohol: no
Wheelchair access: entrance yes; restroom no
Average soup & sandwich plate: $10

Café Malibran is a small and charming café for light meals in Old Montreal.

It's a limited menu but food is beautifully prepared and carefully chosen. The vegetable soup has chunks of vegetables in a light and tasty broth—simple and good. Sandwiches are made with thick slices of country style bread, and they have a good selection including several with Hungarian cream cheese, a delicious pâté, curried chicken, and ham with mint jelly. The sandwich plate includes a generous and very fresh mixed salad that you drizzle yourself with a choice of house dressing (honey/garlic, tarragon, yogurt/mint, or balsamic). Caesar and chicken salads come in both small and large. Espresso is available as are teas made in china pots with loose leaves and a tea ball. For dessert try cheesecake or a simple piece of dreamy creamy homemade fudge!

Marike Carrier and Dan LeBel opened Café Mailbran in early 2002. She's an opera singer and he's a jazzman singer and guitar player. There was an ancient greasy spoon here, and when Marike bought the building they scrubbed away decades of debris. When it didn't rent, they opened their own café. They've created a simple but charming place, definitely *not* a tourist trap. They are experimenting and expanding the menu. They do picnic baskets in summer for tourists. They have many regulars from City of Montreal surrounding buildings, the nearby Archives nationales du Québec, and the municipal court. The café is named after Spanish opera singer Maria Malibran (d. 1808) and her image graces the charming menu and the wall of the café. Come to Café Malibran for soup 'n sandwich or afternoon tea.

Café Presto

1244 Stanley (near Ste-Catherine)
Métro: Peel
Phone: 514.879.5877
Hours: Mon-Sat 11:30am-2:30pm & 4:30pm-9pm;
    closed Sunday.
Credit cards: cash only; Alcohol: beer & wine
Wheelchair access: no
Average main course: $3.95

Café Presto is a budget-friendly cozy little Italian bistro in the heart of downtown.

The wall menu changes every two days, and it offers seven specials, mostly pastas, often including penne arabbiata, linguine paradiso (a creamy rosé sauce) and spicy Italian sausage with tomato sauce. The Presto salad or more modest green salad with house dressing add a fresh touch. Homemade vegetable soup rivals your grandmother's. Food is simple rather than elaborate, but everything is prepared with care and attention and it pleases without fail.

Café Presto is owned by Luciano and Rino Massironi. Rino is the chef and both serve out front. This is a tiny, intimate place with less than a dozen tables pleasantly decked with blue and white checkerboard tablecloths. There are pictures of Marilyn Monroe and James Dean on the walls. Rino or Luciano calculate your tab at the counter and ceremoniously ring a cowbell after you leave a tip. It can be difficult to get a table at lunch during the week—as you can well imagine at these prices in this location. Treasures like this are hard to find in downtown Montreal.

Le Cap Vert

1212 McGill College (at Cathcart)
Métro: McGill
Phone: 514.866.0662
Hours: 10am-11pm daily; closed Sunday during winter
Credit cards: V, MC, Amex; Alcohol: all
Wheelchair access: entrance yes; restroom no
Average main course: $10

Le Cap Vert offers bistro standards with a nod to nouvelle in an intimate and charming downtown spot where the price is right.

Three daily table d'hôte choices are often seasonal specialties—always a good way to go. Salads are a favourite, with an interesting variety of meal-size portions and house-made dressing. The marinière is especially recommended. French onion soup is a wonderful bistro classic, as are Toulouse sausages and creamy coquille St-Jacques au gratin, lightly perfumed with Pernod. Portions are super-generous. Steaks are beyond the *Cheap Thrills* guidelines but there are lots of other things to like. There are pastas and a variety of pita melts. Club sandwiches have rosemary chicken, grilled zucchini and provolone, or smoked turkey breast and emmental—quite a nouvelle twist! Fries are frozen but are good with mayo, and salad is a healthier option. Afternoon tea with homemade cakes is a good shopping break.

The name is a holdover from before the Ros family bought the place in 1982—Cape Verdian food is *not* served here. They enlarged it in 1990 when brother and sister Marina and Lamberto took over. They recently redecorated, adding attractive artist murals of Montreal. There are comfy banquettes along the wall and large windows that provide great views of the passing downtown scene. Service is professional, and pleasant lighting, fresh flowers, and plants add charm. In summer there's a patio and they're open Sundays. Cap Vert is an unobtrusive little treasure downtown, an oasis of calm, good food, and reasonable prices. This is the kind of place you're reluctant to tell anyone about!

La Carreta

350 St. Zotique E. (at Drolet)
Métro: Beaubien
Phone: 514.278.5779
Hours: Mon-Wed 11:30am-10pm; Thur-Sun 11:30am-11pm
Credit cards: cash only; Alcohol: all
Wheelchair access: entrance yes; restroom no
Average snack: *$2; average main course*: *$10*

La Carreta is a neighbourhood restaurant that serves authentic Salvadoran food.

You can make up a very satisfying meal from a number of delicious small snacks like tamales, tacos, enchiladas, and fajitas. They're prepared Salvadoran-style, and are somewhat different from the Mexican versions that are more familiar to most of us. Cilantro and avocado add a fresh pleasing taste to the vegetarian burritos. All the snack foods taste better with the pickled veggies that are a Salvadoran specialty. Don't miss the absolutely scrumptious fried yucca. They put french fries to shame! Don't neglect the house specialty—pupusas— savoury corn flour pancakes stuffed with cheese, chicken, beans, or meat. They're served with a tasty mild salsa or, on request, a more fiery green salsa verde. The pickled cabbage is a must with the pupusas, somehow harmonizing all the flavours and textures. Homemade soups are substantial and satisfying. Large platters of meat or chicken are also available. The food is simple and hearty—down home good if you happen to be Salvadoran.

Jesse and Anna Escobar opened this family business in 1991, serving authentic food from their native El Salvador. Service is friendly and relaxed. It's a bit cluttered and funky with a warm tropical ambiance, cheerful checkered tablecloths, and handicrafts, and there's good Latin music in the background. This is a favourite place for Salvadorans, and for neighbour-hood folks who know a good deal when they eat it!

Casa Gaucho

5834 Ave. du Parc (at Bernard)
Bus: 80 (du Parc)
Phone: 514.270.1300
Hours: 4:30pm-2am daily
Credit cards: V, Interac; Alcohol: all
Wheelchair access: no
Average complete dinner: $15

This Argentinian Grill is a meat lover's paradise on Avenue du Parc.

The specialty here is meat, grilled to perfection, complemented by the house-made special chimichurri sauce. The sauce is so good it's sold by the jar to take out. Soup is life-sustaining, chock full of meat in a tasty broth. Empanadas made here are superb, among the best around town. The real deal though is the grilled meats, available individually or in combinations as complete meals with soup, dessert, and beverage. Portions are very generous and two portions of the special Argentinean grill easily serve three normal people. Beef and pork are tasty, tender, and lightly charred. The sausage is typically Argentinean, half beef and half pork. Boudin is meltingly tender and tasty. Tripe, kidney, and sweetbreads can be substituted if they are not to your taste. You can mix and match meats if you like. The charcoal grill is brought to the table with your chosen assortment and everything is fresh and hot. Salad is ordinary but still a welcome counterpoint. They will do take-out but this food tastes best hot off the grill.

Carlos Sansone came to Montreal in 1968. He worked at Joe's Steak House until he opened his own place in 1973. Since then he has owned and operated several legendary Argentinian places: Rio de la Plato, Argentina 78, Las Brasas, Martin Fiero, and Noches de Tango. He opened Casa Gaucho in 2000 and knows his business. Service is friendly and helpful although it may seem a bit slow at times. Everything is prepared to order, so be patient—it's worth the wait!

Chalet Bar B-Q

5456 Sherbrooke St. W. (near Girouard)
Métro: Vendôme; then 105 bus
Phone: 514.489.7235
Hours: Sun-Wed 11am-11pm; until midnight Thurs;
    until 1am Fri & Sat
Credit cards: V, MC, Interac; Alcohol: beer & wine
Wheelchair access: entrance yes; restroom no
*Quarter chicken with fries, coleslaw, and BBQ sauce: $5.50-$6.50
    at lunch, $6.50-$7.50 after 3 pm*

Chalet Bar B-Q is a Montreal tradition, still going strong in NDG.

They do one thing—rotisserie chicken—and they do it outstandingly well. The quarter chicken lunch special is a great deal. They also serve hot chicken sandwiches and wings. But the overwhelming favourite is beautiful rotisserie chicken cooked to crispy golden perfection with a juicy interior, served with fabulous BBQ sauce for dunking. Fries cooked in vegetable oil are great, but you can have a baked potato if you insist on being virtuous. Depending on your appetite, choose a quarter (leg or breast portion—breast portions are a little extra), a half, or a whole. Predictable but absolutely delicious! The traditional dessert is that 1950s standby, Boston cream pie, but they also serve coconut cream and pecan pie.

These folks have been cheerfully and efficiently welcoming satisfied customers since Marcel Mauron opened Chalet Bar B-Q in 1944. Louise Mauron McConnell (Marcel's daughter) owns it now and Danny Colantonio is the general manager. The décor is knotty pine wood paneling throughout—the cliché Swiss chalet. Booths are comfortable and it's all very relaxed. Single diners, couples, and family groups all feel welcome. Most of the staff are veterans (Lucia Tuccia has been a waitress here since 1952). Service is prompt and friendly, even when they are busy—and they often are. The place runs like clockwork. They do a booming take-out business and deliver without charge. Reception rooms are available upstairs and there's free parking in the rear. There are many imitators but Chalet Bar B-Q is the Real Thing!

La Cheminée

5876 Upper Lachine Road (Clifton)
Métro: Vendôme, then 90 or 104 bus westbound
Phone: 514.481.0123
Hours: Mon-Fri noon-11pm; Sat noon-2am; closed Sunday
Credit cards: V, Interac; Alcohol: all
Wheelchair access: no
Average main course: $12

La Cheminée is a family-run Persian restaurant in NDG.

This menu of Persian specialties hasn't been watered down to satisfy what is perceived as North American tastes. Everyone is served yogurt and raw onions to start. Mirza Ghasemi appetizer is fabulous mashed eggplant with concentrated flavour, served with basmati rice. Main course platters are plentiful, and they include rice, and soup or salad. Soup is a thick, rich bowl of beans, grains, lentils, and noodles, topped with kashk (similar to yogurt) and a drizzle of fried mint in oil—it's satisfying and delicious. The most popular dish is grilled skewers of marinated ground beef with complex and mysterious spicing. It's a Persian classic. The Cheminée special for two includes grilled tomatoes, rice, and three double skewers: filet mignon, smooth and moist chicken chunks marinated in saffron and yogurt, and the marinated ground beef. The marinades are specially created for each dish, and they add depth and complexity to the grilled foods. Each day of the week one of the dishes that requires long slow cooking is featured. Lamb shanks on Friday are memorable. Cardamom tea is refreshing.

Hengameh Ghassemnejad and Ali Sharif came from Iran in 1993. He's a nurse and she's an accountant; but he also cooks and they opened La Cheminée in 1998. It's a large space (two rooms) with subdued lighting, plastic-covered table-cloths and comfortable chairs. It's family-oriented and kid friendly. They have a belly dancer and DJ on Saturday night starting at 10:30. They do take-out and delivery. La Cheminée delivers genuine Persian cooking!

Chez Clo

3199 Ontario E. (cor. Dézéry)
Métro: Préfontaine
Phone: 514.522.5348
Hours: Mon-Fri 6am-3pm; Sat & Sun 6am-4pm
Credit cards: no; Alcohol: no
Wheelchair access: yes
Average special: $8 (*21 choices incl. soup, main, dessert, coffee*)

Chez Clo is a dynamite diner, Québec-style, on Ontario East.

Breakfast is served all day. Daily specials include soup, main, dessert and coffee. All the good things you associate with old-time Québec home-style food are here: roast turkey, Saguenay-style tourtière, ragout de boulettes, salmon pie, pâté chinois (shepherd's pie), and many other comfort foods. Portions are hefty, everything's good. It's hard to beat pudding chômeur (bread pudding) for dessert. It's a little like stumbling into the 1950s. Order bulk main courses for parties or meals at home.

Owner Claudette (Clo) Massé serves unpretentious food, cooked simply and well. She's from Abitibi and she knows about good Québec cooking and that's what she serves—it's real rather than retro! The main eating area has a busy short-order grill behind a long, narrow counter with stools, and booths on the side. Two other spaces seat smokers and there's an outdoor terrace. Service is fast and friendly. This was a run-down neighbourhood when Clo opened in 1982 but things are looking up. This is Hochelaga-Maisonneuve, an old East-end industrial/residential area south of Sherbrooke with small neighbourhood businesses in the optimistic "La Promenade Ontario," a stone's throw from giddy *La Ronde* just across the St-Lawrence River. The resto is across the street from the huge old church of the Nativité de la Sainte-Vierge. The whole area speaks volumes about Montreal history. Eat at Chez Clo and take a look around this fascinating old neighbourhood!

N.B. **Chez Clo is not open for supper**, but it's such a terrific place that we include it anyway. Eat early, do brunch on weekends, or bring home one of their food packs.

La Chilenita

152 Napoléon (at De Bullion)
Bus: 55 (St-Laurent)
Phone: 514.286.6075
4348 Clark (cor. Marie-Anne)
Phone: 514.982.9212
Hours: Mon-Wed 10am-6pm; until 8pm Fri;
   Sat & Sun 10am-6pm
Credit cards: cash only; Alcohol: no
Wheelchair access: no
Empanadas $2 ea; $21/doz; $42.50 for 50; average sandwich: $6

La Chilenita in the Plateau serves tempting empanadas and other Chilean treats.

Some of the best empanadas in Montreal are baked in these two tiny spaces, made by hand daily with the best ingredients and knowing fingers. The dough is perfect—and the pleasing shapes hold the fillings with style and grace. Fillings include chicken, chorizo, sausage, tuna, seafood, and various vegetarian choices. The big winner is the classic beef and onions, accented with black olive and a small piece of hard-boiled egg. It all comes together perfectly, complemented by the homemade salsa. These empanadas make a wonderful snack or a satisfying meal. They serve interesting sandwiches, including a delicious grilled steak with tomato and avocado, and many vegetarian choices. They also have great tacos, enchiladas rojas (with "red" tomato sauce), quesadillas, and some of the best burritos in town. This food is the real thing, not a fast-food look-alike. For dessert try house-made alfajores, sandwich cookies with a caramelly *dulce de leche* filling, topped with coconut.

Both locations are modest and the food is the real draw. Take-out is a big part of their business, including food for parties. Order 24 hours ahead for large quantities. This is such a friendly and unassuming place it's like going to your aunt's house and sitting in her kitchen while she cooks up your favourites.

Chopin

4200 Blvd. Décarie (bet. Duquette & Brodeur)
Métro: Villa Maria
Phone: 514.481.0302
Hours: Mon 11am-6pm; Tue & Wed 10am-6pm;
   Thur & Fri 9am-9pm; Sat 9am-5pm; Sun 10am-3pm
Credit cards: V, Interac; Alcohol: beer
Wheelchair access: yes
Soup & sandwich: $5; pierogi plate $5.50

Chopin is an NDG Polish deli with terrific small meals and homemade pierogi elegantly available on the side.

This is a small Polish deli with a pedigree. There are half a dozen small tables immaculately presented with fresh nappery, real dishes, and silverware for light meals or tea. Everything is made to order and it's all served with panache. Soups are in the hearty Polish style—try zurek or pickle soup for true Polish flavours. Sandwiches made to order with the wonderful deli meats include Black Forest ham, smoked or rolled bacon, Debrezina sausage, smoked pork loin, Kaszanka (blood and buckwheat sausage), and Krakowska. The pierogi are outstanding, a generous portion served with fried onions and sour cream. Many varieties are available: cabbage and mushroom, cheese, blueberry, and meat. Desserts are a real treat: cheesecake, apple cake, Polish donuts, rum balls, cheese Danish, and some incredible seasonal specialties like fruit crumbles.

Eva and Czeslaw Szypura own Chopin. They make most of the meat products themselves and Eva makes the sweets. In addition to great food, you will find many Polish delicacies on the shelves, as well as Polish videos and newspapers. There's a patio for good weather and they are friendly and helpful. It's all so well put together that it's hard to believe it's a deli as well as a resto, and the food is so good you'll want to try it all!

Chuch

4088 Rue St. Denis (at Duluth)
Métro: Sherbrooke
Phone: 514.843.4194
Hours: Mon-Sat 11am-10pm; Sun 11am-9pm
Credit cards: V, MC, Interac; Alcohol: BYOB
Wheelchair access: entrance yes; restroom no
Combo plates including two rolls, rice and main dish: $9.95

Chuch is the veggie Thai express offshoot downstairs from ChuChai on St-Denis.

Chuch is a quick stop for wonderful vegetarian Thai food. The menu is limited, but interesting. There are delightful vegetarian sushi, but the main attraction is a series of combo plates. Combos include two imperial rolls and steamed rice. You can opt for brown rice or noodles for $1 more. Choices for one-person combos include seitan in yellow curry or black bean sauce, eggplant in green curry, an excellent squash stew in tangy red curry sauce, and sautéed tofu. Combos for two include four combinations of two main plates, noodles, and rice. There's quite a medley of tofu, curry, seitan, and veggie dishes. Excellent spring rolls are packed with greens and coriander. Curries are very nicely done. Curry rice noodles with carrots and yams are especially good, as is the seitan with black bean sauce. They have lunch specials that are a terrific deal.

Owners Patrick Michaud and Lily Sirikittikul opened the very successful ChuChai in 1997. In 1999 they opened Chuch where service is efficient, there is a serene atmosphere, dim lighting, decorative tables, and no one rushes you. The ChuChai "complex" includes ChuChai with its upscale vegetarian Thai food; Chuch, a budget-priced vegetarian offshoot; and Centre ChuChai, a health centre for the mind and body, offering tai chi, pilates, yoga, massages, homeopathic services, special workshops, and information sessions. Its message of sane food and lifestyle are complemented by Chuch's excellent high quality food at painless prices.

Congo-Léo

1886 Ontario E. (at Dorion)
Métro: Papineau or 125 bus
Phone: 514.522.1313
Hours: Tue-Thur 5pm-11pm; until 12:30am Fri & Sat;
   Sun 5pm-midnight; closed Monday
Credit cards: none; Alcohol: all
Wheelchair access: yes
Average main course: $10

Congo-Léo on Ontario East serves food from the Congo and West Africa.

The menu is inspired by Africa and the huge country at the heart of the continent, the Congo. Dishes include fish, game, goat, chicken, plantains, rice, manioc, corn and yams—a small, interesting menu and daily suggestions are pulled from it. The origin of each dish is indicated, including Angola, Chad, Senegal, Ivory Coast, and Cameroon. Delicious fried plantain is the accompaniment of choice. Pastille, a crispy, spiced, grilled-meat-filled spring roll, is served with a delicate fresh salsa. Congo-Léo, the house specialty, is an elegant presentation of marinated grilled chicken, light on the chillies, moist and tasty. Makians is a flavour-filled dish of reconstituted salt cod cooked in a tomato and pepper sauce. Also good is the lemon-flavoured chicken yassa, chicken mafé in its peanut sauce, marinated and grilled tilapia with couscous, fresh sardines in Angolan sauce, and Senegalese-style fish with eggplant and carrots. The African tea, made from leaves that are sun-dried, has a fresh, clean taste and aroma.

Gastino Mangala, a native of the Congo, opened Congo-Léo in 2000. He has created a comfortable and welcoming place that is brightly decorated—the original pressed tin ceiling is painted bronze. The terrific Congolese and West African music is great for dinner chair dancing. Tablecloths are lovely Congolese printed cottons, and dishes are simple but colourful. The front window opens in summer. Although it's a little off the beaten track, near the Jacques-Cartier bridge, Congo-Léo is an attractive place with authentic African food.

Coq en Stock

1241 Mont-Royal E. (at de la Roche)
Métro: Mont-Royal
Phone: 514.522.1000
Hours: Mon-Fri 11:30am-11pm; Sat & Sun 11:30am-10pm
Credit cards: V, MC, Amex, Interac; Alcohol: all
Wheelchair access: yes
Average table d'hôte including appetizer, dessert, and beverage: $14

Coq en Stock serves chicken, Island-style, on Mount Royal East.

The house specialty is chicken and they do a mighty fine job of it! This menu provides some interesting chicken variations including a popular house-smoked chicken, grilled chicken with satay sauce, jerk chicken, Thai-style curry, and even a chicken sandwich. Sauces sharpen flavours and add interesting touches. Jerk chicken is a favourite, and the Voodoo chicken is delightful. Chillies have been adjusted to accommodate less fiery tastes so food is not as piquant as one might expect, but you can request extra hot sauce for any of the dishes if you like things really hot. Plantains are good, and you can choose either the traditional Caribbean rice and peas (beans), or fries. A table d'hôte daily special is available and the chicken selection might include a homemade soup like watercress or asparagus vinaigrette, a grilled chicken leg, sugar pie, and coffee. They also have a fish choice on the table d'hôte if chicken is not your passion. Desserts include a wonderful signature key lime pie. They deliver for a small charge.

Pierre Castonguay opened Coq en Stock in late 1999 and he also owns the Pizzédélic branch across the street. He has travelled in the Caribbean and decided that it was time for some of those special chicken tastes to come to Montreal. A wonderful fish tank provides quiet visual entertainment, and they have subdued lighting and some funky tropical accents. There's a casual and attractive tropical feel to the place, ideal for family dining or a special date. They serve Mojitos too! When you crave a budget Island getaway and chicken in all its glories, head to Coq en Stock.

Les Délices de l'Ile Maurice

272 Hickson, Verdun (near Wellington)
Métro: De l'Église
Phone: 514.768.6023
Hours: Mon-Sat 5pm-9pm; closed Sunday
Credit cards: cash only; Alcohol: BYOB
Wheelchair access: entrance yes; restroom no
Average main course: $7

This delightful small restaurant in Verdun serves food with a Mauritius accent.

The flavours of Mauritius are a colourful jumble of Créole, European, Chinese and Indian, with a special place for seafood. As you sit down you are greeted with samosas and delectable deep-fried onion nibblies that you can dip into different salsas. The menu is posted on the blackboard and it changes daily, but the food is prepared fresh and to order, with the exception of the curries. It might include mussels, pork cutlets, chicken, shrimp, squid or scallops, most served with a choice of sauces. The kitchen has a special way with spices, as one might expect. Curries, especially the chicken curry, are exceptional. They turn out a very nice and quite piquant hot sauce.

Flamboyant chef Sylvestre Ng-Kan came from Mauritius in 1980. He worked in Gibby's and in 1995 opened Les Délices de l'Ile Maurice. Primary colours emphasize the tropical ambiance of this small room decorated with posters and maps. You can locate the island paradise of Mauritius in the Equatorial Stream, smack dab in the South Indian Ocean, not too far from Madagascar, east of Africa and south of India. Chef Sylvestre puts on a great show and this place could be billed as dining theatre. Appealing fragrant aromas emanate from the tiny open kitchen. It's very friendly and they are helpful in sorting out what to order. Books on Mauritius are available for browsing while you wait for your meal to be prepared. This is a popular family-owned and kid-friendly restaurant. What a fun way to discover the joys of Mauritius!

Diogènes

925 Blvd. Décarie, Ville St-Laurent (near St-Jacques)
Métro: Côte-Vertu
Phone: 514.747.7251
Hours: 11am-11pm daily
Credit cards: V, MC, Amex, Interac; Alcohol: all
Wheelchair access: no
Average platter: $11

Diogènes is a very popular Ville St-Laurent Greek grill.

Portions are generous and are very easily shared if you don't want to take home leftovers for lunch the next day! Grilled meat and fish are the specialties so it's not a great place for vegetarians. Platters are loaded with salad and rice. Pass on the frozen fries and eat all the salad! The pikilia appetizer selection is a tasty meal in itself, or good for sharing. There is a daily special and it's a popular choice. House specialties are souvlaki, chicken souvlaki, and combo plates. Everything is expertly grilled with just the right touch—you won't find leathery, dried out chicken or fish here! Lightly breaded filet of sole is as tender and moist as is the chicken or lamb. This is a terrific place to go with a crowd and share a bunch of appetizers and different main dishes. Crisp, fresh salads are the ideal complement, but veggies are not their strong point. They do delivery now too.

Diogènes has been a St-Laurent institution for 25 years. Diogenes was a witty and amusing Greek biographer of philosophers (including the hedonistic Epicurus) and he might feel at home in this sunny, casual spot with white walls, and white and blue tablecloths, reminiscent of the Greek islands. Large front windows give the feeling of almost being outdoors. It's consistently packed but you don't feel you've been squeezed into a too-tiny space and the staff doesn't rush you. It's very kid-friendly and there are lots of families, but it works as a date place too. It's hard to believe that anyone would opt for fast food when a place like Diogènes is so clearly a better alternative!

Echalote Restaurant

854 Ste-Catherine E. (near Berri)
Métro: Berri-UQAM
Phone: 514.288.1212
Hours: Mon-Thurs 11:30am-10pm; Fri 11:30am-11pm;
   Sat 4:30pm-11pm; Sun 4:30pm-10pm
Credit cards: V, MC, Amex; Alcohol: all
Wheelchair access: entrance yes; restroom no
Complete dinner special: $10.95

Echalote Restaurant serves a large and varied menu of Asian food on Ste-Catherine near Berri.

The extensive menu includes Chinese, Thai, Szechuan, and Vietnamese dishes. It's really Cantonese cooking with a twist that's Thai, Vietnamese, or Szechuan. Food is cooked to order, so it's hot and veggies are crisp rather than soggy. The combos and specials make an economical choice, and they include soup, crispy imperial roll, main dish, rice, sherbet, and tea. It's hard to beat, especially since the food is actually fresh and good, not steam table casualties. But the à la carte menu has all the dishes you might expect and the kitchen does a good job. The General Tao chicken is far and away the favourite dish—it's outstanding! Hot and sour soup is excellent. Hunan dumplings with peanut sauce add a touch of pizzazz, and Szechuan shrimp are another good bet. Noodle soups are wise and tasty alternatives to meat-packed meals.

Echalote opened in 2001 and it has a clean and appealing décor. Smokers are in the back for a change, and the non-smokers get the windows and a great view for people watching on a busy part of Ste-Catherine. Staff are reserved but friendly—it's quiet here with pleasant background music. They do take-out and delivery. They even have a 10 percent discount for students! (UQAM is close by.) Echalote makes fresh and satisfying dishes that won't startle your palette, and provides a diverse selection of well-prepared food that's easy on the wallet.

El Rincón

7805 St-Laurent (at Villeray – across from Jarry Park)
Métro: de Castelnau; or bus 55 (St-Laurent)
Phone: 514.274.0962
Hours: Mon-Fri 11am-9pm; Sat 10am-11pm; Sun 10am-8pm
Credit cards: none; Alcohol: beer & wine
Wheelchair access: no
Average main course: $10; pupusas: $1.50 each

El Rincón is a hole-in-the-wall with some of the best Salvadoran pupusas in town!

The food is simple and satisfying and the menu is not large. They have meal-size soup, tacos, enchiladas, fried fish, and steak. Pupusas are the important thing here, and they do them beautifully. This stuffed cornflour pancake comes alive with an extraordinarily fine tomato sauce and homemade pickled cabbage that is extra fresh and crisp. Even the black bean filling has a special touch. The tortillas are homemade so they're very fresh and fragrant. Fried fish or chicken platters come with rice, salad and tortillas. The make their own complex hot sauce and it complements just about anything on the menu. There's a student special for local high school students: pupusas and softdrinks for $1 each. What an improvement over fast food chains! Coffee is good.

Blanca opened El Rincón in 2000, coming from Morazzan province in El Salvador, a Central American country smaller than the state of Massachusetts, with six million inhabitants, coastline on the South Pacific, and a long history of earthquakes and volcanos. Corn, rice, beans, chocolate and coffee are major crops and important elements in the cuisine. This neighbourhood across from Jarry Park has many Latinos. El Rincón (meaning the corner) is very basic, kind of like being in someone's kitchen. There are tablecloths covered with plastic, plants, incongruous moose antlers on the wall, and a TV playing Latino soap operas or music videos. It's a family operation—Blanca cooks, her daughter serves, and the 2-year old granddaughter is very much at home here. It's friendly, casual, trilingual. And the pupusas are fabulous!

Elixor

1795 Pierre-Peladeau, Laval (just West of Autoroute 15)
Métro: Henri-Bourassa then Laval Transit bus 61
Phone: 450.687.6877
Hours: Mon-Thur 11am-11pm; until midnight Fri;
    Sat 9am-midnight; Sun 9am-11pm
Credit cards: V, MC, Amex, Interac; Alcohol: all
Wheelchair access: yes
Average main course (aside from steaks/fish/seafood): $11.50

Elixor is a large Chomedy food emporium with a huge
Florida-style menu and gigantic portions.

The 17-page menu details myriad food and drink choices!
They pay attention to quality and sharing is almost required
unless you're breaking a two-day fast! Some appetizers like
the five colossal coconut shrimp with marmalade sauce sound
more like a meal for most people. Pizzas and burgers have a
slew of toppings, something for all. Shepherd's pie is a comfort
food choice as are any of the chicken dishes, especially the
rosemary portobello. Pasta is not overcooked and it comes
with some unexpected fixings, such as peanut sauce with
chicken. Fries are fresh, not frozen, and mashed garlic potatoes
are homemade creamy. Steak, fish and seafood dishes are
beyond *Cheap Thrills* guidelines but it works if you share
(remember portions are big). Salad meals like seared tuna
Niçoise are good choices. The sandwich of choice is the
extravagant Kilo High meat loaf. Brunch is available all day,
and there are weekend specials like corn and crab cakes with
poached eggs, mushrooms and asparagus. Cheesecakes are a
specialty. It's impossible not to find something you like here

George Prontzos opened Elixor in early 2002 with a young,
energetic staff and it was an immediate hit with families and
groups. He's hoping to open another location soon. It's a big
brand new suburban space that still manages to feel stylish
and spacious. It's crowded on weekends but weeknights are
quieter. Groups of six-plus should reserve. Elixor is in the
over-the-top-Florida style so familiar to Montrealers who have
fled there at one time or another to escape the dreaded winter
blahs.

L'Exception

1200 St-Hubert (at René-Lévesque)
Métro: Berri-UQAM
Phone: 514.282.1282
Hours: Mon-Fri 11am-9pm; Sat 11:30am-9pm; closed Sunday
Credit cards: V, Interac; Alcohol: wine & beer
Wheelchair access: no
Average burger: $4.50

L'Exception is a fun burger joint with panache near the Berri metro.

The food here is burgers, but they're quite some burger! They have standard beef, or you can have a variation with buffalo, lamb, veal, or pork. Pick your passion! Burger toppings include dill pickle, tomato, mushrooms, onions, lettuce, mayonnaise, Dijon mustard. For variations add bacon, chile con carne, mozzarella, blue cheese, goat cheese, smoked gouda, emmenthal, cream cheese, or any two-cheese combo you like, and you can mix and match as well. Burgers are good-sized, moist, with flavour, and served on a Kaiser bun. Fries are spectacular: hand cut and fried in canola oil, with just a dash of secret spice. They also have salads and a few croque monsieur variations, but the main event is definitely good meat on a bun dressed to kill.

Guido Tocci and Andreas Parashevopoulos bought L'Exception in 1998. It opened in 1983 and was a favourite hangout of theirs. They jumped at the opportunity to make it their own, and quickly added to the basic menu. Décor is very cool, with old Coke memorabilia, Marilyn Monroe pictures, and other 50s and 60s relics. The walls are painted great colours and have notes from customers written with silver markers—it's a fun personal touch. The smoking room is in the back so it's quite separate from the rest of the restaurant. Sit back and have a burger and fries with a Coke, or do an adult variation with wine or beer. Grab a free gumball at the register to top it all off. Good burgers, good choice, and funky fun too!

Fumoir et BBQ Karl le Gros

89 Donegani, Pointe-Claire (at Sources Rd.)
Métro: Lionel-Groulx; then 211 express bus to Dorval Circle;
    then 203/204 bus to Donegani
Phone: 514.693.1111
Hours: 11am-9pm daily
Credit cards: V, MC, Interac; Alcohol: no
Wheelchair access: yes
Average main course: $11

At last! Montrealers can finally eat southern style American BBQ—in Pointe Claire!

Oh this is good stuff! They call it Texas-style but it's a mix and Southern-style might be more accurate, but no matter! They have deliciously smoky pork and beef ribs, chicken, sausage, beef brisket, and pork. Thank goodness there are combos! It's done with long slow cooking in a proper rig at low temperatures using fresh maple wood. Ribs take 2-3 hours, chicken 3 hours, pork and brisket 12 hours. Beef ribs are sublime—savoury mahogany chunks of meat, tender and juicy inside. Wonderfully moist and tasty pork ribs with a well browned exterior are not masked by a sweet sauce. Smoky, juicy chicken is crisp and brown. Pork is thin sliced rather than pulled or shredded. Sides are important with BBQ and they have coleslaw, a creamy house potato salad, and crisp fries done in canola oil. Dunk in BBQ or mustard sauce and enjoy all that smoky goodness!

Karl Binder is an adventurous Montrealer. In 1982 he bought Scoopy's Ice Cream, moving it to the current location in 1996. He had never eaten southern-style BBQ but he consulted with a cousin who owns Fatso's in Vancouver, bought a rig, experimented, developed his own sauce, and in October 2001 he added BBQ to the ice cream bar and changed the name. Families with kids come here for ice cream in the summer. The BBQ is mostly take-out/delivery. You order your food at the counter, but there are some seats and tables if you can't wait! Definitely worth the trip from far and wide, this kind of BBQ is slow food to die for!

Georgia

5112 Rue Decarie (at Queen Mary)
Métro: Snowdon
Phone: 514.482.1881
Hours: 8am-11pm daily
Credit cards: cash only; Alcohol: no
Wheelchair access: entrance yes; restroom no
Average meal: $14

Georgia offers Georgian, Russian, and Ukrainian specialties in this small place on Queen Mary.

Lunch ($6) includes filling soups, salads, dumplings and blini. There's a basic dinner menu, but more important is what's being cooked that evening. Portions are generous and the host is eager to stuff you in typical Russian fashion, but be firm, three dishes are enough for anyone! Homemade bread is all rye—life sustaining and very hard to find hereabouts. Don't miss the divine eggplant caviar with walnuts and a Georgian spice mix. Satsivi is an enormously popular Russian cold dish of chicken with a sauce of walnuts, cilantro, broth, vinegar, herbs, and spices. Their version is seriously good! Many dishes have beets and other vegetables, cream, coriander, and fenugreek. These people know how to cook so everything is good—be adventurous! Caviar is available if you want to totally blow the budget. Desserts are honey cake, Québécois sugar pie, and real chocolate éclairs.

Yuriy Butrkhrikidze opened this little gem in summer 2002 with his wife Olga. He's Georgian/Ukrainian, and she's Russian. There's only a small bakery sign outside and inside there are eight tables and background Georgian and Russian pop music. This is not the place for you if you're in a rush—there's a relaxed and very agreeable ritual to eating and hospitality. There's no liquor license yet so you have to imagine belting back the vodka! The former USSR was a huge landmass with over 100 nationalities and languages, and this place gives us but a tiny glimpse into the rich and diverse food traditions of this part of the world. Georgia will take you on a leisurely adventure to Russia and the Caucasus.

Govinda Jaya Jaya

263 Duluth E. (at Hôtel-de-Ville)
Métro: Sherbrooke
Phone: 514.284.5255
Hours: Mon-Wed 11:30am-9pm; until 10pm Thurs-Sun
Credit cards: V, MC, Interac; Alcohol: no
Wheelchair access: no
Buffet: lunch $8; evenings $10; weekends $11
Website: www.restogovinda.com

Govinda is an all-you-can-eat vegetarian buffet that serves fresh and satisfying food in a soothing and peaceful environment.

The buffet is strictly vegetarian and is delicious. Selections change but it often includes ratatouille, spiced potatoes and yogurt, vegetables with tofu, chickpea and zucchini curries, papadums, and salads, with semolina or rice pudding for dessert. Everything is extremely fresh, beautifully prepared and simply presented. There is a small but ample selection at lunch, more choices at dinner, and yet more on the weekend. Everything is good but the spinach potato curry and the dahl soup are spectacular. Try a little of everything and then go back for your favourites. You will find things you like even if you aren't a vegetarian.

Govinda is a vegetarian haven. They opened in the summer of 1999, a project of Hare Krishna (although there is no proselytizing). Chef Vicky has cooked in Greece and Egypt, specializing in Mediterranean and Indian food. The food is satisfying and the space is pleasant and unassuming. No smoking is allowed. The chairs are a particular treat—well padded, covered with gold velvet, and with a special back that rolls and somehow feels like a soothing and gentle massage. You can now check the current day's buffet choices on the web site. They deliver free in the Plateau, with a slight charge elsewhere. Presenting positive vegetarian alternatives to the public is what the place is all about and they do it very well.

Le Grand Comptoir

1225 Square Phillips (near Ste-Catherine)
Métro: McGill
Phone: 514.393.3295
Hours: Mon-Wed 11:30am-9pm; until 10pm Thur & Fri;
Sat 12pm-10pm; closed Sunday
Credit cards: V, MC, Amex, Diners, Interac; Alcohol: all
Wheelchair access: no
Daily special: $10.95

The Grand Comptoir is a downtown gem, serving fabulous French bistro fare on Phillips Square.

The daily special (including soup and salad) is a bistro classic like Toulouse sausages, veal in mushroom sauce, or steak-frites. There's also an à la carte menu ($11-$19), including dishes like salmon in wine sauce, calves liver, steaks, cassoulet, and some seasonal specialties. Some are over the *Cheap Thrills* limit but good homemade soup is included, there's variety, and it's good value. Classic salade Niçoise is always a good choice and in winter there is a superb cassoulet made with their own confit de canard served with a special house confiture d'oignon. Desserts are classic French and can include tarte tatin, fruit tarts in summer and blowout profiteroles—a dream come true served on a dinner plate. The special blend coffee is excellent, supplied by Union Coffee on Jean-Talon.

The restaurant opened in 1994 and is owned by Serge, Paolo, and Mario. Their years of experience at Baci and other downtown eateries is evident—they run a terrific kitchen on a shoestring. Be warned, it is crazy busy at lunch and many people eat here nearly every day. Dinner is less frenetic and pure pleasure. Service is polished and efficient. In good weather the large and pleasant covered front terrace overlooking the square is great for people watching. The ambiance is friendly, the food is good, the price is right!

La Hacienda

1148 Van Horne (de l'Épée)
Métro: Outremont
Phone: 514.270.3043
Hours: Tue-Sat 6pm-10pm; closed Sunday & Monday
Credit cards: V, MC, Amex; Alcohol: all
Wheelchair access: no
Average main dish: $11

La Hacienda in Outremont serves authentic but gentle Mexican food and their terrace is one of the best in the city.

Food here is Mexican but tame. Ratchet up the spice if you like. They have a choice of quesadillas, tacos, burritos and enchiladas. The less common chilaquiles are nachos and chicken napped with a choice of delicious sauces, melted cheese, and sour cream. They make things fresh, using quality ingredients, but they hold back on the heat in deference to those who *don't* like it hot! Guacamole has texture, and medium hot salsa is fresh and deliciously chunky. Chicken breast with achiote (deep red annatto seeds), salsa verde, or piquant chocolate molé is a pricier treat.

Brigitte and José Mier y Teran arrived in Montreal in 1986 and opened La Hacienda in 1987, when there was little Mexican food here. He is Mexican and is the chef and she is French and takes care of the front. The restaurant itself is decorated to create a warm ambiance. Service is pleasant and sweet, although it can be a little slow if it's crowded. But you won't care about much if you're sitting on their terrace—a magical place with overhanging grape vines and a plastic curtain that can be drawn to protect patrons from the elements. There are trees and plants on the side and the lighting is soft and pleasant. There's a view of busy Van Horne but it's sheltered from the noise and bustle. What a fabulous place to while away a spring or summer evening with pleasant food, and Chilean wine, Mexican beer, or a couple of Margaritas.

Hoai Huong

5485 Victoria (cor. St-Kevin)
Métro: Côte-Ste-Catherine
Phone: 514.738.6610
Hours: Tue-Sun 11am-11pm, but closed 3-5pm Tue-Thur;
    closed Monday
Credit cards: V, MC, Amex; Alcohol: all
Wheelchair access: no
Average main course: $8

Hoai Huong serves soup and other Vietnamese specialties on Victoria.

There is a respectable selection of pho (noodle) soups that are a meal in a bowl. They include veggies, pork, shrimp, beef, chicken, and Vietnamese sausages. These are light but hearty soups that are both delicious and healthy and always a good choice. The Vietnamese pancakes are a special treat—delicious, light, and served on a large platter with sprigs of fresh mint, salad and dipping sauce. They're addictive! They have many brochettes and wok specialties. The family specials are dishes meant to be shared by large Vietnamese groups where many dishes are ordered; they may not individually have all the pieces for a complete meal (eg.,veggies). The fish in hot pot is utterly exquisite. It arrives in its own well-worn pot and it's simply fish in a sauce to die for with crispy bits of fried garlic. Watch for stray bones and it's very salty but the taste is so intensely delicious you don't care! They have Vietnamese beer (and others), coconut milk drinks, soy milk, and Vietnamese-style coffee with condensed milk.

Hoai Huong is a pleasant little place where you can eat to your heart's content and not spend a fortune. This is not run-of-the-mill formula Vietnamese food.There are great lunch deals and combination plates if that's your style. It's a good place for large groups but is also fine for single diners.

Hwang-Kum House

5908 Shebrooke St. W. (near Clifton)
Métro: Vendôme, then 105 bus
Phone: 514.487.1712
Hours: Mon-Thur 12pm-11pm; Fri-Sat 12pm-12am;
   closed Sunday
Credit cards: V, Interac; Alcohol: all
Wheelchair access: yes
Average main course: $9

This home away-from-home for Koreans in NDG serves a delightful variety of authentic Korean dishes.

The menu includes Korean specialty stews, soups, noodle dishes, and BBQ platters. Everything is served with a delicate soup, light and refreshing marinated bean sprouts, and some of the city's best kimchi—pickled cabbage with garlic and chillies. The savoury green onion and seafood pancake is crisp on the outside, with a delicious stuffing of green onions and squid. Pigs' feet are served in a spicy, sweet sauce. Cold noodles with spicy sauce are a treat that is both cold and spicy hot! Seafood soups are delicious meals in a bowl. The beef ribs are truly wonderful, marinated before being grilled to tender perfection. There are other Korean dishes like soybean stew with vegetables and pork with hot tofu. You will want to work your way through the illustrated menu.

Hwang Kyu-tack and his family run this small place. Two daughters serve out front and cheerfully explain the dishes to the uninitiated. The mother works miracles in open view in the minuscule kitchen. The eating space is snug but comfortable, and they have recently spiffed up the place. The whole operation is relaxed but dignified, and the food is genuine home-style Korean.

Jaarl Paadi

5487 Victoria (near Côte-Ste-Catherine)
Métro: Côte-Ste-Catherine
Phone: 514.738.3881
Hours: Mon-Fri 11:30am-2am; Sat & Sun 11:30am-3pm
Credit cards: cash only; Alcohol: all
Wheelchair access: entrance yes; bathroom no
Average main course: $6

Jaarl Paadi takes over from the Genuine Restaurant to serve Sri Lankan and Indian dishes on Victoria.

Sri Lankan and South Indian food are similar and some of both are offered here. There is a menu but mainly you should order what they are cooking that day. The menu is somewhat in transition with new owners. Some of the specialties are the impressive Madras masala dosa, an 18-inch rolled crepe extravaganza made with fermented dahl and rice, filled with vegetable curry, and served with lentils on the side. Biryanis are a good bet and they have a bit of heat. The distinctive and exquisite Kottu roti includes diced thick Sri Lankan roti added to beef curry. The beef roll is almost addictive. It's a deep-fried breaded oriental wrapper with a curry filling. All dishes are made to order so it can be a little slow—but it's worth the wait.

Jaarl Paadi has just been bought (and renamed) by Sri Lankans Umajothy and Sudan Thambithurai. It is the former Genuine Restaurant owned by the personable Genu Srithoran for eight years. The current chef was trained by Genu and much of the menu will remain the same. It's a tiny, funky place without any décor to speak of, but it's a neighbourhood favourite to sit and chat, and mainly to wait while take-out is being prepared. Call ahead if you want to avoid the wait. It's not really well-organized for eating on site, although the outdoor terrace is a real pleasure in good weather. There are not many openly Sri Lankan places in town although there are many Sri Lankans cooking in Montreal Indian restos. Jaarl Paadi is a bit of an adventure but the Sri Lankan specialties are worth it.

Jamaica Way

4961B Queen Mary Rd (near Décarie)
Métro: Snowdon
Phone: 514.343.5375
Hours: Tue-Wed 9am-10pm; Thur-Sat 9am-11pm;
   closed Sunday & Monday
Credit cards: cash only; Alcohol: no
Wheelchair access: no
Average meal: $10

Jamaica Way serves authentic Jamaican home-style food on Queen Mary.

The day starts with traditional Island breakfast of ackee or calaloo with salt cod. These delicious stews may be a bit of a leap for the uninitiated at breakfast, but try them later in the day. All main dishes come with rice and peas (beans) and salad. Stews and curries are generous servings of meat and vegetables in rich sauces with Caribbean seasoning. Oxtail stew is especially wonderful, with the meat falling off the bone, and a deeply delicious sauce. Jerk chicken is one of the specialties of the house and it's crisp, moist, and aromatic— worth a trip across town! Marinated kingfish is cooked in a sauce of tomato, peppers, and onions, with a dash of heat. Hot sauce is on the side. Rotis are the real thing. Drinks like sorrel are homemade.

Byron Spence, owner, chef, and all-round everything, opened Jamaica Way in 1999. His mom helps out when she can and Jackie is in front. Byron cooks with passion, making fresh food every day. Jamaica Way is popular with both the local business people and with the Jamaican community who come for food they know and love, the background reggae, and the sweet and pungent fragrance of allspice, ginger, and garlic in the air. It's casual, friendly, efficient, and appealing as only a neighbourhood place can be. Reggae king Bob Marley takes it all in from a poster on the wall. There's a party room at the back for smokers and large groups. Jamaica Way is like Kingston, but far from the tourist areas—sidewalk food stands, and hole-in-the-wall restos. Great Jamaican comfort food!

Jardin de Jade Poon Kai

67 Lagauchetière West (near St-Laurent)
Métro: Place d'Armes or 55 bus
Phone: 514.866.3127
Hours: 11am-11pm daily
Credit cards: V, MC, Amex, Interac; Alcohol: yes
Wheelchair access: no
Buffet daily: 11am-2pm ($7.75), 2pm-4:30pm ($6.75), 9pm-11pm ($8.95). Mon-Thurs 4:30-9pm ($11), Fri-Sun 4:30-9pm ($12.25).

This Chinese buffet is a cut above the norm and offers variety and good food at low low prices.

There is a small à la carte menu but the real deal here is the all-you-can-eat-buffet. The broad selection of dishes is superior to most Montreal Chinese buffets. The vegetarian, non-MSG section makes you feel virtuous as you load up on wonderful tofu, vegetable noodles and stir fry. The fresh vegetarian choices are excellent. The regular dishes include a selection of dim sum dumplings, soup, BBQ pork, duck, and chicken, steamed whole fish, spicy shrimp, and numerous other tasty delights. There are western style desserts too, like chewy jello, ice cream and good tiny doughnuts. There is something to please everyone. (Even pizza and pasta if you insist.) The spicy shrimps and the vegetarian choices are particularly good. The food is frequently replenished, and is always hot and fresh.

This restaurant has been in the same spot for 14 years. The space is enormous, the chairs are comfortable, and there are tablecloths and cloth napkins, and a large non-smoking section. Reservations recommended for large groups. Jardin de Jade Poon Kai has a loyal following of Asians and non-Asians and they give excellent value for your dining dollar.

Kei Phat

4215 Jarry E. (near Pie-IX)
Métro: Jarry, then 193 bus eastbound
Phone: 514.376.4590 or 376.5749
Hours: 9am-9pm daily
Credit cards: Interac; Alcohol: food market sells beer
Wheelchair access: entrance yes; restroom no
Average main dish: $8

A no-frills Asian restaurant serving fabulous food in a corner of a food market? Yes indeed!

Instead of a menu as we usually know it, at Kei Phat, you look at colour photos of dishes in a binder—most of the photos have a description and a price but some do not. Basically, you can order whatever you would like and they will cook it for you—and they do it fast and well! You can even choose your fish from the fish counter in the grocery store if you like. The cooks are Thai, Vietnamese, Chinese (Cantonese) and one is from Hong Kong—they are all accomplished and turn out quality Asian food without batting an eyelash. This is home cooking as you might do it if you were Cambodian, Thai, Laotian, Vietnamese, or Chinese. Big favourites are chicken satay, and beef with broccoli and noodles. The Phnom Penh soup is a huge bowl of noodles with your choice of meat. Wonton soup is outstanding—like no other you've ever tasted and so good you could easily make a meal of a large bowl of it! This is not the watery cliché you might expect. Everything is good here and portions are very generous. They do a booming take-out business.

The Tang family arrived in Canada from Cambodia in 1980. After working in textiles, in 1993 they moved into an IGA supermarket space on Jarry. Within six months they had transformed it completely into an Asian market with a 50-seat restaurant. Allow time for shopping from the vast selection of Asian groceries and remedies. Kei Phat is unusual and definitely not glamorous, but it's all about giving your palate a treat!

Kamela Couscous

1227 Marie-Anne E. (near de la Roche)
Métro: Mont-Royal
Phone: 514.526.0881
Hours: 4pm-11pm daily
Credit cards: cash only; Alcohol: no
Wheelchair access: no
Average main course: $9 (prices include taxes)

This small inviting place serves irresistible Italian and North African food—and delivers free in the Plateau.

Kamela has a split personality. Their specialties are Italian and Algerian/Tunisian. There are 27 varieties of pizza with a distinctive and delicious thin crust and all the predictable toppings, plus a delightful homemade merguez. Superb pasta dishes come with tomato, rosé, cream, or pesto sauce. Salads are fresh and nicely dressed. Couscous vegetables are not overcooked and come in a generous, tasty sauce, with plumped raisins and hot sauce on the side. Couscous choices are vegetarian, merguez, grilled chicken (crisp and delicious, not at all dried out), lamb, and exquisite lamb shanks. The halal meats are tender and delicately flavoured. The shanks are roasted, then cooked on top of the stove, and they're worth a trip across town! There are ten varieties of brik: crisp, light, deep-fried pockets filled with fresh, savoury ingredients. There is baklava, sometimes homemade. Fresh mint tea is authentic and soothing. With advance notice they will do special group orders, including tagines, and they also cater. Prices include taxes.

Ali Kara, an Algerian who was formerly involved with Pizza Nostra, started Kamela in 1994 and he stuck to the Italian dishes but added his own North African specialties and touches. There are some very comfortable seats in the restaurant and it's a pleasant place, but almost all their business is delivery and the large and busy kitchen is incredibly well organized and efficient. They deliver very fast and the food is always hot and fresh, even the brik! Kamela is amazingly good for eat-in or take-out, Italian or North African!

Keur Fatou

66 St. Viateur W. (at St-Urbain)
Bus: 55 (St-Laurent)
Phone: 514.277.2221
Hours: Mon-Wed 12pm-8:30pm; Thur-Sat 12pm-10pm;
    closed Sunday
Credit cards: cash only; Alcohol: no
Wheelchair access: entrance yes; restroom no
Average main course: $10

Keur Fatou serves Senegalese/West African specialties and they sometimes feature storytelling and live music too!

Like much West African cooking, the food here relies heavily on peanuts (the main crop in Senegal), and on starches such as plantain, yams, manioc, rice, and couscous. No pork is served. Simple homey ingredients are expertly handled by knowledgeable and caring hands to create classic Senegalese dishes. There are three choices available daily. Chicken mafé is a beautiful mélange of chicken and root vegetables simmered in peanut sauce and served with rice and plantain. Thieboudiene (baked fish) is perfectly spiced and moist, and chicken yassa is a delightful mix of lemon, garlic, onions, and chillies in a rich sauce served over rice. Poisson kaldo is a blend of fresh and smoked fish in onion sauce served with rice and plantain. Homemade hot sauce is available on the side and is added to your taste—if you wish, it will take you all the way to incendiary! Fresh fruit or yogurt are ideal desserts, and homemade ginger juice with a bit of a kick is special.

Ndiouga is the owner, waiter, cook, dishwasher, and storyteller. His wife and friends help out when it's busy. Now and then, after clients are served, he will play a sabar (traditional Woloof drum) and tell stories. Occasionally school groups come by for storytelling, music and snacks— lucky them! They've been open since 2000 in this small space with beautiful Senegalese printed cotton tablecloths. It's comfortable and casual. At Keur Fatou you feel like you've stumbled into a neighbourhood place in Dakar, and it's a place where the food is home cooking good!

Kotori

5468 Ave. du Parc (cor. St-Viateur)
Bus: 80 (du Parc)
Phone: 514.270.0355
Hours: Mon-Sat 5pm-10pm; closed Sunday
Credit cards: V, MC, Interac; Alcohol: all
Wheelchair access: no
Average meal: $10

Kotori, near the Park Avenue "Y," serves quality Japanese food, including sushi and sashimi, at very affordable prices.

The menu includes a selection of noodle soups, from simple egg noodle to fried chicken or shrimp, and fish ball soup. Donbury selections are excellent, and include ten don, a beautifully composed combination of egg, shrimp, tempura, and vegetables including mushrooms, all served on rice. There is a good choice of both sushi and sashimi in 2-piece portions, combination plates of 8-12 pieces, or combo plates of sushi and sashimi. The fish supplier is nearby Nouveau Falero, which also supplies other pricier Japanese restaurants—the quality of the fish is impeccable. Tempura and teriyaki are also good choices. There is a super-value sushi/tempura special on Monday and Tuesday evenings for $9.50! They do take-out.

Owner Yoon-Kee, a Korean, set out to provide authentic high quality Japanese food to Montrealers at reasonable prices when he opened in 1999, and we're fortunate he has succeeded admirably in this simple but tastefully decorated space. His wife Jung Hee handles the kitchen, making the sushi to order, and he takes care of the front with some additional very courteous staff. It all runs smoothly, service is prompt, and it's a very pleasant and soothing place with background Japanese music. Everything is well presented but not in a studied and formal way. These are Japanese diner prices but this is not a diner environment, and the food is in another league. It's high time that Montrealers are able to enjoy Japanese food without breaking the bank! Kotori means "small bird," and you should fly here if you're a Japanese food aficionado without an expense account!

Ma's Place

5889 Sherbrooke Street W. (at Clifton)
Métro: Vendôme, then 105 bus
Phone: 514.487.7488
Hours: Mon-Wed 8am-9pm; until 10pm Thurs; Fri &
    Sat 24 hrs; Sun 12pm-8pm
Credit cards: Interac; Alcohol: no
Wheelchair access : no
850 Décarie (Ville St-Laurent)
Métro : Côte-Vertu
Phone: 514.744.2011
Hours: Mon-Sat 11am-10pm; closed Sunday
Credit cards: Interac; Alcohol: all
Wheelchair access: yes
Average meal: small $8, large $11

Simple and seductive Jamaican cooking is available for eat-in
or take-out in the NDG and Ville St-Laurent locations of this
friendly restaurant.

Lunch specials include a small main course, a homemade
beef or vegetable patty, and a drink. Choices might be fried
chicken marinated in shallots and onions, or jerk chicken in
a special sauce. The soup of the day is a meal in itself. It could
be chicken foot, cow foot, or fish soup on Fridays. Jamaican
specialties like curried goat, salt fish and ackee, or oxtail stew
are wonderful. Most dishes are served with traditional rice
and beans and plantains. Tasty homemade hot sauce packs a
punch and complements the food beautifully and portions
are generous. There's a special Saturday morning brunch of
Jamaican comfort food par excellence. Little home touches
raise Ma's food above the ordinary.

The original in NDG is small but the wall mural makes it
seem like you are cutting through the jungle on a sunny, hot
day. There are four tables inside, with more on the sidewalk.
They also do take-out and delivery. The new VSL location is
larger. Ma (Delma Francis) turned this restaurant over to her
son-in-law Eric Blagrove a few years ago. He had no restaurant
experience. He claims to have learned how to cook from his
Jamaican mother. However it happened, Eric knows what he's
doing, and the food is good, the atmosphere is easygoing.

La Maison des Pâtes Frâiches

865 Rachel E. (cor. Mentana)
Métro : Mont-Royal or bus 29 (Rachel)
Phone: 514.527.5487
Hours: Mon-Wed 10am-8pm; Thurs-Sat 10am-9pm;
    Sun 11am-7pm
Credit cards: V, MC, Interac; Alcohol: wine
Wheelchair access: entrance one step; bathroom no
Lasagne: $4.50/large square

La Maison des Pâtes Frâiches is a take-out or eat-in Italian deli on Rachel.

Hot dishes are set out on a steam table, and appetizers, fresh pastas, and sauces are on view in a deli counter. They have fresh pasta and a variety of sauces—meat, rosé, red clams, some fancy pesto sauces, and an especially fine arabbiata. An impressive selection of antipasti are available by weight: marinated vegetables, fabulous grilled octopus and whole squid, grilled artichoke hearts, Italian-style ratatouille, and olives of all sizes and colours! There's creamy vegetarian and meat lasagne as well as cannelloni, all amazingly good. The lasagne is very popular and disappears fast. The meatballs are large and seriously good! Eat them here or take them home for leftover meatball sandwiches. There is a large selection of imported cheese, and some cold sliced meat.

Francesca Pulizzi opened a small fresh pasta business in 1994 after the grocery store the family had in Park Extension for 21 years burned down. It took off and sons Roberto and George, and Danny Sodano joined in. Dad sells quality fruit and veg next door. They offer a nice range of things, including prepared dishes, but also fine olive oils and vinegars, mustard, crackers, coffee, French and Italian cookies and many other specialty items. The eat-in facilities are pretty basic but it works for a meal on the run. You can gather enough ready-to-heat-and-serve food here for a solo meal or a fine dinner party, or you can sit at the counter or tables at the front of the store and eat a delicious meal. It gets quite crowded at meal times, but it's fun to combine food shopping with a meal or a snack.

La Maison du Bedouin

1616 Ste-Catherine W. (Le Faubourg at Guy, 3rd floor)
Métro: Guy-Concordia
Phone: 514.935.0236
Hours: 11am-9pm daily
Credit cards: cash only; Alcohol: no
Wheelchair access: yes
Average main course: $6

This is an oasis of North African food in a most unlikely setting—a fast food stand in Le Faubourg mall!

The Bedouin's House continues to expand its menu and provide delicious food that's a little different. Daily specials with salad and rice come with succulent meatballs in a rich gravy, merguez sandwich, a vegetarian plate chock full of various stewed goodies, and a delectable pastilla with almonds, chicken, and a hint of rosewater. During the colder months harira is available. This life-sustaining chickpea soup traditionally breaks the Ramadan fast. Chicken and veal tagine are tasty Moroccan stews with rich gravy served over saffron rice or couscous. Lamb merguez is mild and savoury. Combo plates allow you to taste more than one thing and they're a good bet. They use halal meat. Turkish coffee is available, but the real winner is the mint tea— made the proper way with fresh mint in a metal pot, and served in charming traditional tiny glass cups. There is a small selection of pastries but the freshly made donuts are irresistible. Ask for some honey on the side to make them even more delectable!

Khalil, the Moroccan owner and chef, has created a small but diverse and authentic North African menu in this compact and well organized food mall stand. This is a great place for lunch when Le Faubourg is busy, but it's also very pleasant in the afternoon or evening when it is quieter. Moroccan mint tea is a great choice any time.

Malhi Sweets

880 Jarry W. (near Wiseman)
Métro: Parc, then bus 80 (du Parc) or 179 (L'Acadie)
Phone: 514.273.0407
Hours: 11am-11pm daily
Credit cards: cash only; Alcohol: beer & wine
Wheelchair access: entrance yes; restroom no
Average main course: $6.50

This Jarry Street resto serves delicious Sikh-style Punjabi food.

Some of the selections are unusual combinations so stretch your wings and enjoy yourself. The channa samosa appetizer is an unexpected pleasure, with a base of samosa pastry topped with a mixture of chickpeas, potatoes, green peas, onions, tomatoes, yogurt, and the whole thing finished with chutney. The lamb curry is a favourite. Other good bets are the chicken tikka and the saag paneer spinach with mustard, onions and ginger. The dahl makhani is a great vegetarian choice of black kidney beans in a rich sauce of garlic, butter, and ginger, with an unusual spicy edge. There is a selection of nan bread and it pairs well with the food. No pork is served of course, and vegetarian dishes are available. One of the main attractions is the sweets, eat-in or take-out ($5/pound)—they have a great selection.

This family business began as a small dessert counter and it expanded into a full restaurant with sweets. Owner Burnamm Singh Malhi began with recipes from his wife and his mother. Although they now have a cook, it is still a friendly family business. Decoration is minimal except for the wall hangings with pastoral Indian scenes.A huge standing fan keeps things cool in warmer weather. Bollywood movies on satellite TV add a note of authenticity! Kids are welcomed here and everyone loves the food.

Mango Bay

1202 Bishop (bet. Blvd. René-Levesque and Ste-Catherine)
Métro: Guy-Concordia
Phone: 514.875.7082
Hours: Mon-Wed 11:30am-10:30pm; until 11pm Thur & Fri;
   Sat 3pm-12am; Sun 3pm-10pm
Credit cards: V, MC, Amex, Interac; Alcohol: all
Wheelchair access: no
Average main course: $11; *Roti*: $7; *Early-bird special*: *$8.95*

Mango Bay serves authentic Caribbean specialties downtown in a converted Victorian house.

Jamaican sensibilities shine through the cooking and house specialties include all the standards. They have excellent jerk chicken, and roti is done extremely well—a delicious handful. They have fishcakes, curry goat, ackee and saltfish, and they even make their own sour sop. The signature chicken has a smooth mango sauce, and the house salad dressing has a lovely hint of mango too. Rice and peas (beans) and plantain come with almost everything. Hot sauces include a hot Caribbean blend, and a house version that may blow your head off! They have great lunch specials and an early-bird special (main course and soup or salad) every day between 3 and 6 pm for an incredible $8.95! The table d'hôte of the day is a good choice, but it's sometimes over the *Cheap Thrills* limit. Vegetarian dishes are available but this is not their strong point. The cheesecake is made especially for them and it is served with mango coulis.

Courtney Allen and Rupert Edwards (chefs from Jamaican Pride), Lydia Moore, and Sid Giber (he owns the building) joined forces to open Mango Bay in the summer of 2001. It's an attractive and charming space in a converted 1890s limestone house with gorgeous stained glass windows. Island bands play live on Saturday between 6 and 9 pm. Service is friendly but remember this is not fast food and they need time to make many of the dishes to order. Mango Bay delivers dressed-up charm with a casual touch, but make no mistake—this downtown kitchen also delivers the goods on real Island cooking with a Jamaican twist!

Mavi

5192 Gatineau (bet. Queen Mary & Jean-Brillant)
Métro: Côtes-des-Neiges
Phone: 514.340.9664
Hours: Mon-Wed 11am-10pm; Thur-Sat 11am-11pm;
    closed Sunday
Credit cards: cash only; Alcohol: all
Wheelchair access: 2 steps at entrance; restroom no
Average main course: $10

Mavi serves perfect Portuguese charcoal-grilled meats and fish at amazing prices.

The specialty is grilled chicken, lovingly basted with homemade hot sauce and cooked over charcoal until it is smoky, crisp, and juicy. Depending upon how hungry or how greedy you are, choose a quarter, a half, or a whole chicken. Meals are served with fresh salad, and fries or rice. The fries are cut in-house and cooked in vegetable oil—really good. They also serve platters of Portuguese sausages, pork, beef, and ribs. Fish choices include cod, sardines, squid, shrimp, salmon, swordfish, and trout. Everything is grilled, everything is great! If you insist on the mundane, you can order a hamburger, but don't do it! Sumol is a refreshing Portuguese soft drink that is a good counterpoint to the food; they also offer six Portuguese wines, and an expanded selection of beer. You can order brandy and port, and there is still one lonely bottle of Johnny Walker Red Label on the shelf. But Mavi is more about eating fabulous grilled meat and fish than it is about drinking.

Maria Goa opened Mavi in 1997. She runs the place and husband João does delivery and helps out between runs in the evening and on weekends. They arrived from Portugal in 1987. Young son Michael is a cheerful presence. Mavi does a booming takeout and delivery business. They have painted and done some renovations but this is a very basic space and it can get smoky from the grill. Ah, but the food is something else altogether!

Mazurka

64 Prince Arthur E. (just east of St-Laurent)
Métro: Sherbrooke; or 55 bus (St-Laurent)
Phone: 514.844.3539
Hours: Mon-Fri 12pm-10pm; Sat 11am-10pm; closed Sunday
Credit cards: Interac; Alcohol: no
Wheelchair access: entrance yes; restroom no
Specials with soup, main course, and beverage: $6-$6.75

The Mazurka serves Polish comfort food and it's one of the best deals in town.

This is how your mom would cook if she were Polish. The special is $5.75 on weekdays and $6.75 on weekends, and it features pierogi, blintzes, potato pancakes, meat or vegetarian platter, or Polish sausages. This bargain price includes great homemade soup and tea or coffee. It's impossible to spend a lot of money here, even with the à la carte specialties like Wiener schnitzel, salmon steak, chicken Kiev, osso bucco, or the perennial Mazurka favourite, goulash. Everything tastes like home cooking and portions are generous. Desserts are crème caramel, cakes, and cheesecake. Wine is available at very reasonable prices.

Stanislaw Mazurek opened the restaurant in 1952 on St-Laurent Boulevard, and it moved to its present location in 1964, amid plumbing and sandal shops. Now part of a trendy strip, it is run by Mazurek's daughter Josephine and her son Mark. The Mazurka "family" includes veteran servers like Zutka and Grace who have been there for decades, as have many of the patrons. It is now a large establishment with 180 seats, four levels, and a terrace section. The atmosphere is informal and relaxed, with folksy paintings of the old country on the walls. Service is friendly and extremely efficient.

McKibbin's Irish Pub

1426 Bishop (bet. De Maisonneuve & Ste-Catherine)
Métro: Guy-Concordia
Phone: 514.288.1580
Hours: 11am-3am daily
Credit cards: V, MC, Amex, Interac; Alcohol: all
Wheelchair access: no
Average main course: $9

McKibbin's is a downtown Irish pub with all the trimmings, including very good food.

The food complements the bar of course, but in the best pub tradition you can get good food and good value. This kitchen is not an afterthought and they pay attention to quality. The menu (in an old newspaper format) includes the story of the ghost of Mary Gallagher, old ads, a history of the red sandstone building itself, and other interesting bits. House specialties are Irish stew (with lamb), fish and chips, and burgers. The buffalo burger is a juicy, tasty, low-fat delight smothered in browned onions! Shepherd's pie and steak and kidney pie have tasty fillings ensconced in a flaky homemade crust. Chef Christophe Ritoux regularly features Cajun specialties like crab cakes and jambalaya. Set daily specials (salmon steak on Monday, prime rib or fried trout on Friday) or the chef's special are always a good bet. Fries are real, not frozen, and they're terrific. There are 16 imported beers and the house brew on tap, and you will also find a bountiful selection of single malt scotch.

Dean McKibbin and Rick Fon opened McKibbin's in 1997, but it feels like it's been there forever. It's all the things a good neighbourhood pub should be—warm, friendly, inviting, with good food and a well-stocked bar. A mix of Irish and contemporary bands plays in the evenings, and there's a back terrace in summer. It's quite crowded for after-work drinks but not unpleasantly so. McKibbin's is a congenial and affordable downtown spot—with good food too!

Le Pavillon Nanpic

75A de La Gauchetière W. (near St-Laurent)
Métro: Place d'Armes
Phone: 514.395.8106
Hours: Mon-Fri 11:30am-12am; Sat 1pm-12am;
    Sun 12pm-12am
Credit cards: V, MC, Amex, Interac; Alcohol: all
Wheelchair access: no
Average main course: $9; average complete meal: $13.50;
Peking duck: $29

Nanpic has a Cantonese and Szechuan menu in a casual and attractive Chinatown space.

Nanpic (meaning North and South—Canton and Szechuan) has a full menu (rather than a staggeringly large one) and it's well organized and clear. Won-ton ravioli with peanut sauce and a hint of hot is mouth-watering, a real winner! General Tao chicken (a perennial favourite) is extremely good, with over a dozen pieces of juicy chicken in a crisp batter, and a sauce that is sweet and as spicy as you want it. The kitchen produces dishes that are fresh, tasty, and plentiful, with vegetables always crunchy and fresh. They are one of the few places that always have Peking duck (three courses) on hand. The first course is duck sliced thin with crispy skin intact, ready to be rolled up in small paper-thin warm pancakes with scallions and hoisin sauce. The second course is a duck and vegetable stir-fry. Be sure you get the finale, duck soup! Peking duck feeds two very comfortably, but supplement with another item if you are three.

The Yung family came from Hong Kong in 1983. They opened Nanpic in 1988 in this location and brother/sister team Dennis, Joseph (the chef), and the ever-smiling Dorothy run it as a family business. It's a long and narrow downstairs place, with an intimate atmosphere, low ceilings, white walls, and recessed lighting, classy but informal. Chairs are comfortable and not placed like sardines in a can, and mercifully it's not as noisy as most places in Chinatown. Nanpic is consistently heads above the norm!

Le Nomad

2110 St-Denis (at Sherbrooke)
Métro: Sherbrooke
Phone: 514.282.8744
Hours: Tues-Sun 5:30pm-11:30pm; closed Monday
Credit cards: Interac; Alcohol: all
Wheelchair access: no
Average main course: $13

Le Nomad on St-Denis has good couscous with an Algerian touch.

Traditional Algerian food includes Berber, Arab, and French influences. You find tastes of cumin, coriander, cinnamon, mint, and fennel, and food is hot or not. Le Nomad's Chorba is a light and tasty Algerian soup made with tomato, chickpeas, coriander, couscous, veggies, vermicelli, and topped with fresh mint. Merguez made here is mild—half lamb, half beef. There are also tagines and brik on the menu but the house specialty is couscous in all its glory. Add to the perfectly cooked couscous their delicious vegetable mixture with lots of tasty liquid and if you wish, meats of your choice and a dash of harissa for this classic North African dish. Chicken is beautifully grilled but moist and tender, and merguez are wonderfully tasty. But the real winner is lamb shanks. They are large, tasty, and tender—thrice-cooked apparently. However they do it, it works beautifully. Couscous Royal combines chicken, merguez and lamb shank. It's a large portion that can certainly be shared by two, especially if it's combined with an appetizer, or you can take some home. The homemade baklava is quite different from the ordinary, with cinnamon and other spices and it's lovely lightly drizzled with honey. Mint tea is properly prepared with fresh mint and gunpowder tea, and served in metal pots and elaborately decorated tea glasses from France.

Native Algerian Makhlouf Ouarab came to Canada in 1990, and he opened Le Nomad in 2000. He is committed to cooking Algerian-style. It's a tiny unpretentious place with Algerian decorations, and staff are very friendly and helpful. Come to Nomad for a pleasant North African experience.

"No Name" Restaurant

9700 St-Michel Blvd. (below Sauvé)
Métro: Sauvé, then 129 bus east
Phone: 514.389.6732
Hours: Mon-Fri noon-2:30pm; Mon-Wed evenings by appointment only; Thurs-Sat 7-10pm (*Reservations essential*)
Credit cards: cash only;   Alcohol: all
Wheelchair access: no
Prices: antipasto $10/person; pastas $10-$16

This restaurant without a name on Boulevard St-Michel uses the best possible ingredients in affordable pasta dishes.

At this wonderful and quirky place you can spend a little or a lot. The food is so good you may blow your whole restaurant allowance! The antipasto is a meal in itself, and the more you are the better. It's seasonal but might include olives, grilled peppers, eggplant, artichoke, mushrooms, prosciutto, lonza, pepper-studded cheese, and lightly grilled crusty bread with a drizzle of olive oil. You could stop here, but you might not! Excellent dried pasta (better than poor quality "fresh") is served with extraordinarily fine sauces, Italian style. Sauce coats lightly, pasta isn't drowning in a too-rich stew so you taste all the layers of flavour. Tomato/basil sauce is almost ethereal, sundried tomato/pancetta is savoury, truffle/artichoke has a wonderful sharpness, and porcini sauce is the ultimate. They have excellent meat and fish main courses but they're beyond the *Cheap Thrills* guidelines. As always, Illy coffee is pure pleasure.

Luigi Totarella began as an importer of quality foods, including specialized mushrooms. He and son Tony now both also cook in this little place with a basic interior; ably assisted by Moroccan Chaldy. The utterly charming sheltered terrace has overhanging grape vines. Some of the imports are available for sale. This is a very special place with fine food sensibilities, and respect for quality. The bill can add up quickly but the food is divine, especially anything with mushrooms (their specialty). There is no sign and no name, the menu is limited and market-inspired, but this Italian countryside trattoria produces some of the finest Italian food in the city.

Nonya

1228 St. Laurent (at Ste-Catherine)
Métro: St-Laurent
Phone: 514.875.9998
Hours: Tue-Fri 12pm-3pm & 6pm-10pm; Sat & Sun 5pm-10pm;
   closed Monday
Credit cards: V, MC, Interac; Alcohol: no
Wheelchair access: entrance yes; restroom no
Average main course: $9

Indonesian cooking is finally available to Montrealers at Nonya on Lower St-Laurent Boulevard!

Nonya got off to a bit of a slow start but they're ironing out the kinks and the menu is expanding as they become more established. The food is Indonesian home cooking all the way with some charming touches of panache in the presentation. Flavours from tropical Indonesia, the largest archipelago in the world (13,000 islands, over 200 million people!), include ginger, lemongrass, coriander, cumin, chillies, coconut milk, galangal, lime leaf, tamarind, peanuts, garlic, cardamom, nutmeg, turmeric and shrimp paste. Rice is the staple. Hot sambals are on the side. Specials at Nonya are market driven, therefore unpredictable, but intriguing, and some may make it onto the regular menu. Laksa soup and the grilled shrimp on mango are absolutely wonderful! Grilled chicken with rice, and fried noodles with shrimp, chicken and marinated cukes are good choices. They don't use MSG. Food is fresh and refreshing, with little bursts of heat. Tea comes in a huge mug. Like more familiar Thai food, Indonesian cooking is complex and layered, full of flavour and stimulation for the palette. Be adventurous and try it all!

Ivan Wiharto and sister Stephanie opened Nonya in May 2002. Their mother checks in regularly with advice and recipes from her Jakarta restaurant of the same name and logo! They've used burlap and lots of space to create a pleasing minimalist look. It's attractive with a modern edginess. The Lower Main location was inspired—the space is large, it's central, and there's a very mixed clientele. At last Montrealers get to eat real Indonesian food—and it's gooood!

Pattati Pattata

4177 St-Laurent (at Rachel)
Métro: Mont-Royal
Phone: 514.844.0216
Hours: Mon-Fri 9am-11pm; Sat & Sun 11am-11pm
Credit cards: cash only; Alcohol: beer only
Wheelchair access: no
Average burger plate: $5; single burger: $1.50

Patati Patata is a really neat little snack bar on St-Laurent Boulevard in the Plateau.

This is a casse-croute menu with attitude! They have breakfast, hamburgers, tofu burgers, poutine, fish and chips, club sandwiches, borscht (yes, borscht!), and roast beef made fresh daily! Burgers are small—great if you want a little less indulgence, especially if you add cheese and bacon. If you're really hungry you might want a hamburger plate and an extra burger. Plates come with fries and a salad with add-your-own sun-dried tomato or sour cream/basil dressing. The tofu burger is terrific, with garlicky hummus—a nice touch! Shoestring fries done in peanut and canola oil are divine— try adding a squeeze of lime. Poutine is an uptown version with mushrooms, onions, peppers, and chicken gravy with wine. And there's a meat version too. They have a Mediterranean burger with feta and mint, and even a Montignac-style hot dog with cabbage, carrots, and cheese! There are 15 burger toppings—tick them off on a special checklist. Homemade brownies and Queen Elizabeth squares are super yummy. They have *real* fresh orange and grapefruit juice and beer by the glass or pitcher.

Louis Dumontier gave up carpentry and opened this tiny place in 1996 when he turned 40. It's small and cramped, with three tables, a counter with seats and an open kitchen. Service is fast and friendly. They play a unique and eclectic mix of music, old and new—jazz, reggae, funk, soul, r&b, blues, rock, folk, bluegrass, house… There's often a lineup and it can be smoky and noisy, but it's a cosy spot with good food, great music and a colourful clientele!

Le Petit Alep

191 Jean-Talon E. (at de Gaspé)
Métro: Jean-Talon
Phone: 514.270.9361
Hours: Tue-Fri 11am-11pm; Sat & Sun 9:30am-7pm;
    closed Monday
Credit cards: V, MC, Amex, Diners, Interac; Alcohol: all
Wheelchair access: yes
Average main course: $12.50 (Prices include taxes.)

This Middle Eastern bistro on Jean-Talon east is a pocket version of its celebrated parent right next door.

The menu includes many Syrian/Armenian dishes, redolent of cumin, coriander, cayenne, and garlic. Leisurely brunch is available Saturday and Sunday until 3 p.m. Lunch specials include soup, salad, and a main dish, which might be fish, or artichokes stuffed with chicken. It's always a good bet to order a selection of dishes and share. The vegetarian plate includes rich and creamy hummus, puréed eggplant, a delectable vibrant red spread of pomegranate and nuts, stuffed vine leaves, beet salad, lentils and rice—ideal for two to share as a first course. The sabanegh (spinach with spices in a grilled pita), with or without cheese is one of a medley of delightful appetizers. The special lamb is available as a plate or a sandwich. It is cooked all day to create a wonderfully rich and delicious stew. Kebab osmally is a beef brochette slathered with tahini, garlic, nuts, and spices, and available as a plate or a sandwich. Try anything that tickles your fancy, this kitchen does not disappoint. Flavours are complex and the food is authentic.

The Frangié sisters Tania and Chahla, whose family owns the very popular Restaurant Alep next door, run the Petit Alep. Mother Jacqueline cooks for both places. This food is prepared with love and lots of experience. Service is very friendly. This is a great place to have a quick meal, or to linger over good food and a wide choice of coffee or tisanes.

Phad Thai

5045 Wellington (at 5th Ave.)
Métro: De l'Eglise
Phone: 514.761.7149
Hours: Tue-Thur & Sun 4:30pm-10pm; Fri & Sat. 11:30am-
   10pm; closed Monday
Credit cards: cash only; Alcohol: no
Wheelchair access: no
Average main course: $7.50 (Prices include taxes)

Phad Thai is a modest place in Verdun with heavenly traditional Thai food.

It's a big menu and it's all good! Most dishes are available with chicken, pork, shrimp, beef, seafood or vegetarian variations and the kitchen is very accommodating. Spring rolls are compact, crunchy and fresh. Every mouthful of the curried chicken coconut soup packs a different taste explosion! Pad Thai is the usual litmus test for Thai cooking and theirs passes with flying colours. This is not a steam table special. It's made to order as it should be, with crunchy sprouts and peanuts, soft and perfect noodles, chicken, shrimp, bits of egg, and perfect seasoning—it's spectacular! Red and green Thai curries have still crunchy veggies with duck, chicken, pork, beef, or shrimp in unctuous sauce. Thai fish cakes with lime leaves are the pièce de résistance, not available elsewhere in Montreal. The tastes are clean and complex with lots of kaffir lime, coriander, coconut milk, lime, and chillies, but above all everything is fresh, fresh, fresh!

Father and son team Manas and Ronnawee Sirichayaporn opened Phad Thai in fall 2001, committed to cooking traditional Thai food, rather than pale westernized imitations. Manashoo is over seventy, a tea expert with more than forty years of cooking experience in Thailand, and Ronnawee has worked in hotel kitchens and dining rooms in Thailand. The place itself is basic Chinese diner, with bright fluorescent lights, but nobody cares—this restaurant is about heavenly food! Get yourself to Verdun for some of the best Thai food in town!

Pho Bang New York

970 St-Laurent Blvd. (cor. Viger)
Métro: Place d'Armes, or 55 bus
Phone: 514.954.2032
Hours: 10am-9:30 pm daily
Credit cards: cash only; alcohol: no
Wheelchair access: no
Average soup: $5

Pho Bang New York is an unpretentious Vietnamese soup place at the edge of Chinatown.

There is a large selection of pho, or noodle soups that are a complete meal in a bowl. A basic beef broth is the base to which are added endless combinations of noodles, meat, fish, tofu, vegetables, and topped with fresh herbs. It all cooks quickly, adding to the taste and texture of the bubbling broth. It's a light, low fat, and healthy mix that satisfies hunger without leaving you feeling like a blimp! Soup comes in small, large, and extra-large. The extra-large is humungous, perfect if you're a lumberjack! On Saturday and Sunday there is a special spicy soup available—for those who want to spice up their weekends. Beware, it creeps up on you and it's hot stuff indeed! Crispy fresh spring rolls make a good accompaniment to the soups. Vietnamese ice coffee is an ingenious curiosity—poured over condensed milk. If you still crave a sweet ending, the Dragon beard candy store is close by.

Owner Nguyen Thank Phong came here from South Vietnam in the 1980s. She handles the front and her sister, who graduated from a Vietnamese culinary academy, very ably handles the kitchen. This is not a place to linger. People move in and out quite quickly. The décor won't win any prizes, but it seems perfect for this food—comfortable and without pretentions.

Pizza Cachère Pita

5710 Victoria (at Côte-Ste-Catherine)
Métro: Côte-Ste-Catherine
Phone: 514.731.7482
Hours: Sun-Thur 10am-11:30pm; Fri 10am-3pm (one hour
   before sundown); Sat 1hour after Shabbat-3am
Credit cards: V, MC, Interac; Alcohol: no
Wheelchair access: no
Large falafel: $4.50; Falafel plate: $6.25 (Prices include taxes)

Pizza Cachère Pita is a frenetically busy kosher restaurant that
serves fabulous falafel and other Middle Eastern staples.

   Falafel sandwiches here rival the best street food of Tel
Aviv—large pita pouches stuffed to overflowing with falafel
balls, red cabbage, lettuce, chickpea salad flavoured with
cumin, cucumber, tomato, dill pickle, and a generous
sprinkling of sumptuous fried eggplant, all dressed with
tahina sauce, and optional hot sauce. Eating falafel can be a
messy business but who cares when it's this good! Order the
falafel plate if you insist on being proper, but be warned it
somehow doesn't taste the same when it's not dripping all
over the place. There is no meat here, only dairy, so the pizza,
hot dogs, and poutine are all vegetarian. They've recently
added Tunisian sandwiches—a great combo of tuna, black
olives, mayo, onion, and special spices on a baguette. You can
even get a mock kebab in a pita or fried filet of sole. Pizzas are
dressed to taste with olives, peppers, pineapple, artichoke,
heart of palm, eggplant, tuna, and anchovies. Many people
come just for take-out. You can also reserve the party room
downstairs.

   Israeli-born Chaim and Tzvi Spiegelman keep the whole
operation simple and fresh, making the food to order. You
don't have to keep kosher to love the food here. Despite the
fast food ambiance, they've got all the elements right and the
food is delectable.

N.B. **They are closed on all Jewish holidays**—call ahead to
verify.

Première Moisson

490 Sherbrooke W. (near Mackay) plus 12 other branches
  including public markets and Central Station.
Métro: Guy-Concordia
Phone: 514.931.6540
Hours: Mon-Wed, Sat & Sun 7am-7pm; Thurs & Fri 7am-8pm
Credit cards: V, MC, Interac; Alcohol: beer
Wheelchair access: yes, if you call ahead
Daily special: $6.95

This downtown French-style bakery café serves delightful light
meals and extravagant pastries at very modest prices.

The special of the day includes a light main course like
quiche, salmon pie, or provençal tart, salad, a light dessert,
and coffee. They also serve a daily soup such as cream of
vegetable. The sandwiches are on some of the best bread
around—roast beef, bocconcini with pesto and tomato on
olive bread, ham and cheese, and other charcuterie tasties.
Don't overdose so you can indulge in the pastries. There are
fabulous opéra cakes, mouth-watering fruit tarts, pear/
almond tarts, millefeuilles, lemon tart, crème brulée, and a
breathtaking array of other delights in the Le Nôtre style,
including some delightful seasonal specialties. Everything is
made fresh here and it's all available to eat in or take out.
Coffee is excellent and microbrewery beer is also available.

Première Moisson is a terrific bakery that grew—but it has
found the magic recipe to rigorously maintain its high
standards in all its locations. It is wildly popular and justifiably
so. They also have an exquisite selection of house-made pâtés,
quiches, and other French favourites—other branches offer
different possibilities (and have different hours). The
Sherbrooke Street branch has a delightful terrace that is ideal
for people watching. Inspired breads, homemade charcuterie,
fabulous pastries, good coffee, and prices you couldn't dream
of in Paris. How can you go wrong?

Puca Puca

5400 St. Laurent Blvd. (near St-Viateur)
Bus: 55 bus (St-Laurent)
Phone: 514.272.8029
Hours: Winter: Tues-Thur 5:30pm-9pm; until 11pm Fri & Sat;
     closed Monday. Summer: noon-2:30pm
Credit cards: Interac; Alcohol: all
Wheelchair access: no
Average table d'hôte: $12 (Prices include taxes)

Puca Puca serves wonderful Peruvian food in a warm and inviting atmosphere.

Some of the best food here is the fish and seafood, befitting the cuisine of a country with more than 1,500 km of Pacific coastline. The table d'hôte includes soup or salad, main course (usually three fish selections), dessert, and coffee. Grilled shark is exceptional. Ceviche could be considered the national dish of Peru. The high-protein grain quinoa, sometimes called Inca rice, occasionally appears on the menu. Fish is always very fresh and the kitchen cooks it with a sure hand! Grilled marinated beef heart is a particular Peruvian specialty (usually served with cold potato), and it is delicious, although not always available. They do rabbit in spicy peanut sauce and the veal jambalaya is particularly good. Potatoes are native to Peru and several varieties are used in many dishes. Desserts are made in-house and include crème caramel and Queen Elizabeth cake.

Energetic owner/chef Ciro Wong wanders in and out of the kitchen to mingle with the patrons. He opened here in 1995. The name Puca Puca resonates in many ways for Ciro. It reminds him of his hometown, Pucalpa, in the Peruvian jungle, and his father's restaurant there. The name has other connections too, including the chicken dish called puca. The restaurant is a large, open area decorated with Peruvian artefacts. Service is polite and prompt, the atmosphere relaxed and unpretentious. Puca Puca is popular with families and groups. It's a friendly introduction to Peru and its food.

Pushap

5195 Paré Avenue (cor. Mountain Sights)
Métro: Namur
Phone: 514.737.4527
Hours: 11am-9pm daily
Credit cards: cash only; Alcohol: no
Wheelchair access: yes
Average main course: $5.50

Pushap is a wonderful bustling restaurant that serves home-style vegetarian Punjabi food.

They serve a full range of vegetarian dishes—and they're all great! The thali special of the day offers two choices of curry with dahl, rice, and one of several types of Indian breads, and it's always a good bet. They have what may be the best samosas in town, served with tamarind sauce—utterly divine and addictive. Their own paneer goes into several wonderful dishes. Outstanding curries include potato/yam, and eggplant/tomato, but you won't go wrong with anything on this menu. Chapatis and parathas are ideal accompaniments. Spices are handled with a deft and knowing hand, and ingredients are fresh, fresh, fresh! Sweets are homemade by the father and there are always at least a dozen choices, including milk cake, ladoo, barfi, and wonderful gajrela (carrot cake). Sweets are available for take-out at $4.50 a pound.

Daljit Mohan and members of his family, look after the front. His mother and other family members produce the great Northern Indian vegetarian cuisine. They recently closed the West Island branch and enlarged the Paré premises, so it is a little less crowded and there is more space for the take-out line, but it's still busy at peak times. There is no smoking. Service is always friendly, and although things sometimes get harried, the food makes it all worth it. You don't have to be vegetarian to like this food. Pushap is worth a trip from whatever part of town in which you may be—this food is GOOD!

Quartier Perse

4241 Decarie (cor. Monkland)
Métro: Villa Maria
Phone: 514.488.6367
Hours: Mon-Thur 12pm-3pm & 5pm-10pm; until 11:30pm Fri;
    Sat 5pm-11pm; Sun 5pm-10pm
Credit cards: V, MC, Interac; Alcohol: all
Wheelchair access: no
Daily special: $9.50 in the evening

This elegant NDG restaurant offers sophisticated Persian food.

The food is truly authentic and there are all kinds of delightfully unfamiliar dishes that are obviously home-style cooking done with flair and care. This place doesn't offer much choice for vegetarians. You can make up a tasty vegetarian meal from appetizers such as yogurt with wild Persian garlic, eggplant/tomato/garlic dip, an unusual but flavourful eggplant and whey dip, but the rest of the menu is for meat-eaters. The soup is wonderful and is almost a meal in itself. The daily special varies and it could include as a main course a wonderful beef stew with split peas and tomato rice, chicken stewed in a rich walnut and pomegranate sauce, or beef with kidney beans in a *fine herbes* sauce. The tender lamb shanks in a tangy lima bean sauce are excellent, as is the chicken breast marinated in lemon and saffron before grilling. Rice with tangy red Persian berries (zershk) is memorable! (Zershk are available in Middle Eastern groceries if you wish to try it at home.) It's fun to try things you've never eaten before, especially if they seem like unlikely combinations, and here they almost always turn out so it's a double delight! The cooking is refined and the tastes are complex and interesting.

Mahin Kalantary is the owner-chef and her husband is the manager. They have created a tastefully decorated space with paisley tablecloths and discreet music. Smokers and non-smokers are in separate rooms. They have a small outdoor terrace. Quartier Perse is a quintessential cheap thrill!

Quatre Saisons

4200 St. Jacques W. (near St-Phillipe)
Métro: St. Henri
Phone: 514.932.3309
Hours: daily Sat 11am-11pm
Credit cards: V, Interac; Alcohol: all
Wheelchair access: no
Average main course: $9

Quatre Saisons in St-Henri specializes in Korean specialties cooked at the table.

Meals begin with six delicious appetizers to whet the appetite and amuse your palate before the main event. House specialties are Korean barbecue and shabu shabu. They bring a special cooker to the table for the BBQ, along with what you have ordered—beef, chicken, pork, tripe, or prawn. It can get a bit smoky but it's well worth it. Wrap the cooked meat in lettuce leaves and sauce and enjoy! This is good stuff! Shabu shabu was developed (so the story goes) by Genghis Khan to feed his troops quickly and efficiently. Bite-size pieces of meat/fish/seafood and veggies are swished by each diner in a "hot pot" of boiling broth until food is cooked to your taste. The final course is the soup which has become richer and tastier! They also serve spicy codfish soup, cold noodle soup with seafood, and spicy beef stew. The spicy dishes can be very hot, but you can request less heat. The menu includes Japanese specialties but most people stick with the Korean dishes. They have great lunch deals. Beautiful carved oranges for dessert are refreshing and complimentary.

Souk Soon Park opened this family business in 1998, and she is also the chef. She previously had a restaurant in Vancouver. Décor is not the strong point, but it's comfortable and casual, with really neat private booths for larger parties. There's a good feeling here, and ample room between tables. Staff are friendly, helpful, and attentive although language is sometimes a problem. This is some of the best Korean food in town and it's fun too!

Roi du Plateau

51 Rachel W. (at Clark)
Bus: 55 (St-Laurent)
Phone: 514.844.8393
Hours: Mon-Sat 5pm-10:30pm; Sun 5pm-10pm.
   Reservations suggested.
Credit cards: V, Interac; Alcohol: all
Wheelchair access: entrance yes, restroom no
Average main course: $13

Le Roi du Plateau serves glorious Portuguese grill in the Plateau.

The menu contains nothing but Portuguese grill specialties, both seafood and meat. Everything is cooked fresh to order, portions are enormous, and there is not an item on this smallish menu that isn't delicious. Grilled squid is out of this world, possibly the best in the city. The centrepiece at Roi du Plateau is the grilled chicken. It's moist and tender, perfectly spiced, smoky, and the skin is crisp and golden—a cut above the rest. The fries are wonderful. Pork with clams is a traditional Portuguese combo and if you've never tried it you're in for a treat. Shrimp, cod, clams, quail, pork, lamb— all grilled and all great. The grill guys are masters at what they do. Your only problem might be what you will not be able to choose. Vegetables are not a strong suit—a simple salad is as far as it goes. Vegetarians should try their luck elsewhere. Portuguese beer or wine goes really well with everything. They do *not* do takeout, preferring to take care of in-house customers properly in a limited space.

Monica and Michel Viegas came to Canada in 1970. He worked at Doval, and they opened this in 1997, with daughter Katia helping as well. They are very amiable and clearly happy that people enjoy themselves immensely here. It can get very busy and very noisy, and there are times when you just can't get in. It's not a fancy place, but it's perfect for a fun evening out rather than a romantic rendezvous. Every night a Latin guitar player/singer shows up and plays an eclectic mix of Latin songs and requests. Le Roi du Plateau is a real winner!

Trattoria La Rondine

5697 Côte-des-Neiges (near Côte-Ste-Catherine)
Métro: Côte-des-Neiges
Hours: Mon-Fri 11am-11pm; Sat & Sun 4pm-11pm
Credit cards: V, MC, Interac; Alcohol: beer & wine
Wheelchair access: no
Average table d'hôte: $12 (including soup, salad, main course)

La Rondine is an Italian trattoria hiding on a busy corner in Côte-des-Neiges.

The menu has all the usual Italian specialties but the food is a notch above the norm. The daily table d'hôte has terrific choices. Pasta is unfailingly cooked al dente and served in hefty portions. Match your choice of non-formula sauce with fettuccine, penne, spaghetti, or linguini; for $1 more have ravioli, tortellini, or fresh polenta. Pasta riccia della casa is dressed in olive oil and garlic, exhuberant with sun-dried tomato, fresh peppers and broccoli. The arrabbiata sauce packs a punch, lasagne with small meatballs is very popular, and the rosée sauce is sensuously smooth. Rotola, a baked pasta roll with spinach and ricotta sets a high standard! All-you-can-eat mussels marinara (served with pasta) are a deal! Veal and fish dishes are available on the nightly table d'hôte. They serve good Italian coffee.

Paul Casullo opened Trattoria La Rondine in 1994, going from real estate to restaurant, based on the fabulous homecooking of his wife Maria. She makes the desserts and fans claim her tiramisu is better than sex! Rondine is on the busy intersection of Côte-des-Neiges and Côte-Ste-Catherine, but it's tucked away quite unobtrusively, above the Café République. This is *not* a snack bar, despite the location. There's a small outdoor terrace. They have cloth napkins and tablecloths and it's perfect for an evening out without breaking the bank. It's busy at lunch, and people from the nearby hospital are regulars. Service is professional and quick and they're kid-friendly. You can't go wrong at this quintessential trattoria: an agreeable and reasonably priced place where the kitchen can be trusted with Italian homestyle cooking.

Rococo

1650 Lincoln (bet. Guy & St-Mathieu)
Métro: Guy-Concordia
Phone: 514.938.2121
Hours: Tue-Fri 10am-10pm; Sat 11am-10pm;
    closed Sunday & Monday
Credit cards: V, MC, Amex; Alcohol: all
Wheelchair access: no
Average main course: $8

Rococo serves mouth-watering Hungarian food.

The menu includes many Hungarian specialties. Portions are large, but the leftovers are good too! The plump fragrant cabbage rolls full of juicy flavour have a nicely spiced filling of rice and meat. Cabbage noodles and noodles with egg are the stuff of comfort food dreams. Chicken liver with onions and sweet paprika is a big favourite, followed by chicken paprikash and the goulash. Salad dressing is deliciously sweet and tart. Soups are filling and delicious like your grandmother always said they should be. They also have a delicious and nutritious healthy menu created by Dr. Joe Schwarcz. Dr. Joe's vegetarian goulash is incredible! It's low-cal but filling, a secret recipe with tofu and an unbelievable sauce. Vegetarian mushroom goulash with an egg on top is also a great choice. The vegetarian options are so good that you won't even be aware you're being virtuous! Maybe the best thing they make is the yummy Hungarian pancakes, palacsinta, with a chocolate sauce with secret ingredients that surely comes from another planet. You'll fight over the last drop! The cakes are divine indulgences. This is authentic Hungarian comfort food.

Rococo opened in 1996. The Pragai family arrived from Hungary in 1988. Jyorjyi is the chef, husband Jozses is the pastry chef and son Tamas is out front. It's a pleasant and comfortable place, with an outdoor terrace. They are unfailingly friendly and helpful. Some regulars eat here Tuesday through Saturday; it's varied, good, economical, and you definitely won't leave hungry. Rococo serves Hungarian home cooking that just makes you feel good!

Rotisserie Panama

789 Jean-Talon W. (near d'Outremont)
Métro: L'Acadie or 80 (du Parc) or 92 bus (Jean-Talon W.)
Phone: 514.276.5223
Hours: Fri-Sat 11am-1am; Sun-Thurs 11am-midnight
Credit cards: V, MC, Amex; Alcohol: all
Wheelchair access: yes
Average main course: $11 *(Prices include taxes)*

Rotisserie Panama is a no-frills Greek grill-house, offering generous portions of meat and potatoes, served with a smile.

The kitchen prides itself on quality fresh ingredients. All the appetizers are great and you can make a meal of them if that strikes your fancy. Order a combo or a selection for a large group as part of the mix of things you might all share. The grilled octopus appetizer is the stuff of dreams! There are several full-meal platters of souvlaki, chicken brochettes, and pork chops, served with salad, potatoes, and rice. Whole grilled chicken with all the trimmings for two is a wonderful buy and you can thoroughly enjoy a pound of baby lamb chops for two. On Friday and Saturday treat yourself to succulent spit-roasted lamb ($19/pound) but get there early, they *always* run out! All the meats are cooked with a knowing and respectful hand and everything is tender-smoky-good. Fries are hand-cut and great. Grilled fish and seafood are twice the price of the meats, but good value if you want to splurge.

Service is sassy but efficient, and the décor is vaguely Greek blue and white. Owner Jimmy Dimitrios and his manager daughter Tina keep things lively and entertaining. Rotisserie Panama has nothing to do with Panama, the canal, or the hat. The name comes from the former owner who lived in Panama before coming to Montreal. This is a popular family spot and kids are welcome but it's also a good choice for a late-night meat and potatoes feast.

Rumi

5198 Hutchinson (at Fairmount)
Bus: 80 (du Parc)
Phone: 514.490.1999
Hours: Mon-Fri 10am-11pm; Sat & Sun 10am-midnight
Credit cards: V, MC, Amex, Interac; Alcohol: all
Wheelchair access: entrance yes; restroom no
Average main course: $8

Rumi in Outremont has a constantly changing menu from around the world.

This is an eclectic menu with regional food specialties from the Mediterranean, the Middle East, Africa, and the Orient. Portions are large. The Israeli sandwich is a lunch favourite. Soups constantly change. The Iranian eggplant appetizer is a delight! Lamb is very popular; it's grilled, with yogurt, saffron, fresh mint and spices. The main dishes are very substantial portions including basmati rice or home fries. There are desserts such as coconut squares, Turkish delight, and honey with yogurt—simple and sane endings to a meal. These food tastes come from all over the world and you get to mix and match as you please.

Chef Todd, his brother and some friends opened this resto in November 2001, inspired by studying the poet Rumi, an eighteenth century Afghan poet. Todd has travelled extensively and he studied cooking at the NY Culinary Institute of America. He also learned about food from his grandmother. The kitchen has expertise across a whole range of cuisines. He keeps the menu rolling along, and if you like the food sensibilities, you'll probably like to check out the new things the kitchen is trying. It's a different approach to setting a menu, following flights of fancy and pursuing interests. It's big, open, and nicely decorated, with well-spaced tables, plants, and subtle lighting. You can eat here often and not get bored. It's quite a United Nations of tastes and aromas.

St-Viateur Bagel & Café

1127 **Mont-Royal E.** (at Christophe-Colomb)
Métro: Mont-Royal
Phone: 514.528.6361
Hours: 6am-midnight daily
Credit cards: Interac; Alcohol: all
Wheelchair access: yes
5629 Monkland, NDG
Métro:Villa Maria, then 103 (Monkland) bus
Phone: 514.487.8051
Hours: 6:30am-midnight daily
Credit cards: V, MC; Alcohol: all
Wheelchair access: yes

The legendary St-Viateur bagel is now available on Mont-Royal East *and* on Monkland—and it's all dressed!

St-Viateur's brick-oven-baked bagels are available to take out or to eat here. The hot item is bagel sandwiches, with a strategically-placed lettuce leaf so the generous filling doesn't slip through the middle! Selections include egg and tomato, egg and ham, and traditional smoked salmon with cream cheese, These bagels are tender, slightly smoky, chewy, and utterly fresh —as you would expect them to be. There is just a hint of sweetness from a quick pre-baking honey-water dunk. This is, after all, the quintessential Montreal bagel, not a glorified bread roll with a tiny centre. Sandwich bagels are made fresh to order, salads are great, all ingredients top quality. There's coffee, of course, and the desserts are very good (especially cheesecake), if you're so inclined.

Vince and Nick Morena started rolling bagels as teenagers. Vince made a deal with dad, Joe, owner of the landmark St-Viateur Bagel,to licence the name and recipe. He took two bagel makers with him in 1996 when he opened the café on Mont-Royal where centre-stage is a huge wood-burning brick oven in which some of the world's best bagels are baked. It worked, so well that he and his brother opened another on Monkland. People love the food and the coziness of both places where you can linger over coffee, or read magazines from the selection available. The bonus is you can take warm St-Viateur bagels—Montreal's finest—home with you too!

Sandwichmania

23 Mont-Royal E. (at St-Laurent)
Métro: Mont-Royal or 55 bus
Phone: 514.281.0400
Hours: Mon-Wed 11am-7pm; Thurs-Sat 11am-midnight;
    closed Sunday
Credit cards: no; Alcohol: all
Wheelchair access: yes (small step)
Average sandwich: $5; empanadas: $2.25

Sandwichmania is a tiny Latino sandwich joint with great sandwiches, salads, and empanadas.

Sandwich fillings include grilled beef, chicken or pork, ham, cheddar cheese, black olives, avocado, tuna, and mushrooms in various combinations. Very generous portions of filling are placed on a crisp, light, Portuguese bun. The tuna salad sandwich is stylishly and tastefully dressed with thick slices of avocado and black olives. Meal-sized grilled chicken salad is way beyond the run-of-the mill: fresh romaine lettuce with still-crisp green beans and avocado are topped with a hefty portion of grilled strips of moist chicken. The lemon-infused dressing is fabulous! Empanadas are baked daily on the premises and they have a thin, perfect crust—with beef, chicken, artichoke, or spinach fillings. Beef empanadas are the best bet; the moist filling has chunks of meat, the standard small slice of hardboiled egg and olive, and lots of plain good taste. Salsa is mild but good. Fajitas are also available. They serve beer, wine, coffee, and hot chocolate.

Owner Gerson Munoz opened Sandwichmania in 1998. There's a board outside with menu items featured. There are only six tables and six stools along a wall counter—it's jammed at peak times but many people do take-out and they do delivery during the week. Latin music keeps the place hopping, and it's a friendly place for a beer and a bite late at night on the weekend. Choose your food at the counter, and eat in or take out yummy light meals.

Sans Menu

3714 Notre-Dame W. (near Bourget)
Métro: Lionel-Groulx
Phone: 514.933.4782
Hours: Tue-Fri 11:30am-10pm; Sat 5pm-10pm; Sun 5pm-9pm;
  closed Monday
Credit cards: V, MC, Interac; Alcohol: all
Wheelchair access: yes
Table d'hôte: $14.50-$18.50

This jewel of a place in the middle of working-class St-Henri is an unlikely spot for fine French bistro cuisine.

The blackboard menu features a bistro-style selection of main dishes with soup or salad. Main course selections might include poulet citron (delicately lemon-flavoured breast of chicken) served with French-style homefries, house specialty salade farfelue (strips of smoked salmon, feta cheese, and prosciutto over vegetables and greens), perhaps rabbit or salmon with seasonal vegetables. Some selections are beyond the *Cheap Thrills* guidelines but go ahead and blow the budget if you can manage it, it's great value! There are also à la carte items. Microbrewery beers and a good selection of reasonably priced wines are also available. They have lunch specials too.

Despite the neon signs of the pharmacy across the street, a charming atmosphere prevails. Colette Marchessault and partner Pierre Baudin opened the restaurant in 1993. Pierre runs the kitchen and Colette handles the front. Service is fast, friendly, and efficient, and the food is fabulous. This is a great choice for a special romantic evening. At Sans Menu you get quality French cuisine at good prices—and it comes without the snobbery!

Santangelo's Sandwicherie Italienne

2350 Guy (at Sherbrooke)
Métro: Guy-Concordia
Phone: 514.937.7444
Hours: Mon-Sat 11am-7pm
Credit cards: cash only; Alcohol: no
Wheelchair access: no
Sandwiches: $5.25-$7.50; pasta: $4.50-$7.50 (Prices include taxes)

Yes!!! Real Italian sandwiches downtown—and Santangelo's has pasta too.

Oh, these are fantastic sandwiches! Porchetta, Italian sausage, veal roast, grilled chicken—they're all good but favourites are sausages made here and flavour-packed porchetta. They come with provolone cheese, lettuce and tomato, hot peppers or pickled eggplant; mayo or mustard is optional. Where to start? Everything is homemade. Quality meat is cooked as you would do it at home, eggplant pickle is to die for, hot peppers are suitably zippy and tasty, and fabulous bread (especially the ciabatta) is from Lola's in St-Léonard. It's a dynamite combination! There are two sizes, a reasonable size on a Kaiser bun, and an oversize on ciabatta. You can have a salad too. They've recently added pasta with their own tomato or pesto sauce. You can have meat or cheese ravioli, fazzoletti, or manicotti; potato gnocchi are cooked fresh on order. Pastas are from Mike and Dominic's Villa du Ravioli in Rivière des Prairies. Of course there's Brio, San Pellegrino, Mauro Italian coffee, and biscotti. Did we mention it was Italian?

Jon Carlo (JC) Santangelo from Laval opened here in December 2001, originally with a partner who made great sandwiches at his butcher shop. He's alone now and following the business plan he developed in a an entrepreneur class at Vanier College. It's a nice little place a few steps down on Guy at Sherbrooke, with a counter where you order your food and tables with comfortable chairs. No luxury, it's a sandwich place—but it's clean and comfortable. They'll stay open later if there's a demand. If you love authentic Italian sandwiches you'll find these irresistible!

Schwartz's

3895 St-Laurent (near Duluth)
Bus: 55 bus
Phone: 514.842.4813
Hours: Mon-Thurs 9am-12:30am; until 1:30am Fri;
    until 2:30am Sat; Sun 9am-12:30am
Credit cards: cash only; Alcohol: no
Wheelchair access: entrance yes; restroom no
Smoked meat sandwich, fries, & soda: $7.40; rib steak + fixings,
$12.95

Schwartz's on the Main is Montreal smoked meat at its best—maybe even Montreal at its best.

Schwartz's Hebrew Delicatessan is justly legendary for smoked brisket that is juicy, tender, perfectly spiced. It tastes divine. The classic meal choice is a sandwich, fries, and a dill pickle, washed down with a black cherry soda. Medium (fat) has the perfect proportion of fat to lean. Sandwiches are made of piping hot, expertly hand-cut meat piled high on fresh sourdough rye bread. Fries are freshly made, cooked perfectly in vegetable oil. Pickles are Mrs. Whytes—try the half sours. Smoked meat platters are available for those who don't want to do the sandwich juggle, but they're huge and definitely less fun! There's an open charcoal grill and they charbroil a terrific rib steak with a small side order of liver and a frank if you are feeling ravenous. You can take out sandwiches, cold meat by the pound, or smoked chicken. Smoked ducks and turkeys can be ordered during holiday seasons. The smoking and spicing are faultless, and it's all done without preservatives!

Schwartz's has an old-time deli atmosphere all its own—narrow and cramped with barely enough room to move. There are long lineups on weekends but it's always worth the wait. Staffed by veteran waiters, the service is quick and efficient. The distinctive Rumanian-style smoked meat has become known as "Montreal" smoked meat, the standard against which all others are measured. It's often brought, on request, to far-flung parts of the world to provide expats and one-time visitors with a Montreal fix. IT DOESN'T GET ANY BETTER THAN THIS!

Shish-Kebab

9394 Blvd. De L'Acadie (near Chabanel)
Métro: Bus 179 from L 'Acadie métro
Phone: 514.858.6222
Hours: 11am-12am daily
Credit cards: V, MC, Interac; Alcohol: all
Wheelchair access: yes
Average grill platter: $10

Restaurant Shish-Kebab near the Marché Central has excellent grilled Lebanese kebabs and other specialties.

All the grill platters include salad, hummus, rice or fries, and pitabread. The tasty filet mignon shish kebab platter is a real winner (two or three kebabs). They are even better as leftovers in a sandwich! Shish taouk and ground meat kebabs are neither undercooked nor dried out. There is an interesting fish tagine appetizer. Tiny homemade Lebanese sausages cooked in lemon are outstanding! Hummus is faultless, and the smoky, silky baba gannouj may just be the best in the city! Vegetarian options include some interesting cheese specialties. Fries are hand- cut on site and fried in canola oil—lovely! You can also get grilled chicken and various sandwiches of grilled meat. Small whole onions grilled kebab-style are a nice touch. There are great lunch specials. There's baklava of course for dessert.

Toufic Nakhoul and his wife Françoise emigrated from Lebanon in 1999 with his parents. He had a restaurant in Lebanon for six years and opened Shish-Kebab in 2000. It's a family operation with everyone involved cooking, serving, and hosting. The mother cooks, and the brother does the grill. It's spacious with lots of light, free parking in front, and they're always working at upgrading the interior. They do takeout and delivery. They're open late and lots of people come from nearby Chabanel after working late or after shopping at Winners, Club Price, or Réno-Dépôt just across L'Acadie. This is a perfect food stop for great grilled kebabs and that memorable baba ganouj!

Smoked Meat Pete

283 1st Ave (at Perrot Blvd, Ile Perrot)
Phone: 514.425.6068
Hours: Sun-Wed 9am-11pm; Thur-Sat 9am-1am
Credit cards: cash only; Alcohol: beer & wine
Wheelchair access: yes
Sandwich, fries, slaw, pickle, and soft drink: $7

Smoked Meat Pete serves top quality Montreal-style smoked meat on the West Island.

The main event is definitely the smoked meat, but Pete's also offers a respectable range of deli foods: sandwiches such as smoked turkey breast, salami, stuffed chicken, chopped liver, and bagels with cream or Swiss cheese. They also serve rib steak and a chicken and ribs combo platter. They have sides of dill pickles, potato latkes, potato salad and really good hand-cut fries. Homemade apple pie and cheesecake are provided by Pete's mom Julia Santini and they're good if you have room. But this is Montreal and the crucial question for a deli is "How's the smoked meat?" The consensus is that it's very good indeed—coming close to Schwartz's, which is the standard against which everyone else is measured in Montreal. Pete's has natural smoked goodness, and it is tender and juicy. Order a medium if you want just the right proportion of fat to lean. Spicing is good and the meat is hand cut, as it should be.

Smoked meat runs in the family. Owner and chef Pete Varvaro opened Pete's on the West Island after working with his dad, who owns The Main on St-Laurent. They've moved around a bit. In 2000 they moved to a bigger and better space on Ile Perrot. Brother Pete opened Deli-Bee, a small place at 24 Valois Bay in Pointe-Claire with a more limited menu but the same smoked meat. This is a good West Island deli with terrific smoked meat.

Soy

5258 Blvd. St-Laurent (at Fairmount)
Phone: 514.831.2822
Hours: Tues-Thurs 11:30am-2:30pm; 5pm-10:30pm;
    Sunday 5-10:30pm; closed Monday.
Credit cards: V, MC, Amex; Alcohol: all
Wheelchair access: no
Average table d'hôte: $14

At last, Soy is back again to serve irresistible pan-Asian food!

Soy, on St-Denis near Duluth, opened its doors in 1999, and was held in high esteem by many faithful clients, young and old, until it was destroyed by fire in June 2001. Many have mourned the absence of this stylish, modern, but casual place. There have been difficulties and they have finally abandoned hope of re-opening at the old site. Soy will soon open on the Main where, we are assured, they plan to keep the same concept.

The personable Manny Cheng takes care of the front and the talented Suzanne Liu works her inspired magic in the kitchen. The menu will be much the same, but we await new additions, such as a range of innovative maki rolls, with baited breath. Manny and Suzanne both come from cosmopolitan Hong Kong. He has been in Montreal (via San Francisco and Toronto) since 1976; Suzanne came to Canada as a child. He worked in hotels, she in restaurants, and they both ended up at Zen doing management. Suzanne always cooked herself but was never able to cross the invisible glass barrier into the Asian restaurant kitchen. In 1999 they opened Soy, where they served dishes they loved to eat themselves. Their years of hospitality experience and Suzanne's well-developed culinary abilities combine to create the magic of Soy.

The new Soy menu will include their spectacular saké-infused chicken, a divine appetizer of shrimp wrapped in daikon with a basil ginger dip, tender and succulent Korean BBQ beef short ribs, and their deliciously-different version of General Tao chicken in a light and crispy batter with a subtle ginger/lemon flavour. We know there will be noodle dishes. We're anxious to see what else they will come up with!

La Strega du Village

1477 Ste-Catherine E. (at Beaudry)
Métro: Beaudry
Phone: 514.523.6000
Hours: Mon-Fri 11am-midnight; Sat & Sun 4:30-midnight
Credit cards: V, MC, Interac; Alcohol: all
Wheelchair access: yes
*Average table d'hôte (including soup or salad, main course and
  beverage): $10*

La Strega du Village is a charming resto for a wonderful Italian
meal in the Gay Village.

Combine your choice of al dente homemade pasta with
any of the fine sauces. Choices include arabbiata, Alfredo,
pesto, red or white clam, puttanesca, and matriciana. Lasagne,
manicotti, cannelloni, and tortellini are also available. Add
sausages, artichokes, mushrooms, or smoked salmon for a
small premium. Pastas are always cooked to order, and the
quality is consistent, with fresh parmesan added to taste. Gigi
with prosciutto, mushrooms, and white wine is a house
specialty. The table d'hôte includes some pasta dishes, fish,
and meat choices. Veal choices are excellent and the prices
are unheard-of elsewhere. Salad is fresh with a house dressing.
Appetizers are wonderful and can be put together for a meal.
This isn't exciting and trendy food: they consistently produce
quality versions of standbys like pasta arabbiata, beef
Bourguignon, and veal with mustard sauce. There are no nasty
surprises—quite the reverse, given the modest prices.

Antonio Kelada (a native of Calabria) had a resto in Genoa
before he came here in 1980. He opened the wonderful
L'Amalfitana in 1986 near Radio-Canada and sold it in 2000.
In 2000 he renovated an old fast food place and opened here.
It's intimate, with old-fashioned charm, red walls, cloth
tablecloths, and an eclectic choice of Italian background
music. But most important, Antonio is in the kitchen! They
are accommodating and service is efficient, although it slows
down at peak times. We can thank Antonio for offering his
wonderful food at such affordable prices!

Tao

3741 Victoria Ave., Westmount
Métro: Vendôme
Phone: 514.369.1122
Hours: Mon-Fri 11am-10pm; Sat & Sun noon-10pm
Credit cards: V, MC, Interac; Alcohol: all
Wheelchair access: no
Average table d'hôte: $13.95

Tao offers serves wonderful Chinese food in a lovely Westmount resto.

The menu is varied but the kitchen shines with Cantonese. The table d'hôte has 12 selections that include appetizers, main dish, rice, and dessert. The General Tao chicken is a particular pleasure and very popular. Other good bets include hot and sour soup with shiitake mushrooms, mu-shu chicken with hoisin sauce, scallops with ginger and garlic, orange ginger beef, eggplant with red chilli bean paste, and vegetarian tofu pot. They have Peking duck with mandarin pancakes if you want a special indulgence. Grilled salmon with black bean sauce is also terrific. Don't miss the King Tao chicken or the squid in salt and pepper. In fact, the only problem is too many good things! Portions are generous and presentation is aesthetically pleasing, with carved vegetables decorating the plates. Food is cooked fresh to order, and spiciness can be adjusted to taste. They serve Szechuan and Thai too, but go for the Cantonese. Complimentary almond cookies and honey-roasted almonds make a fine ending.

Tony Yung opened Tao in 1999. He grew up in the restaurant business; his family owns the Nanpic in Chinatown. He does some of the cooking, with three other chefs. Tony is very hands-on and it really makes a difference. He attends to all the little details that make dining a pleasure. Tao is nicely decorated and elegant, with white tablecloths and cloth napkins, but they still manage to keep the prices reasonable. This is a good kitchen and they are very accommodating so don't be shy. At Tao the food is great, prices are very reasonable, and it's charming too!

Le Tropico

9153 Pie-IX (cor. 47th St.)
Métro: Pie-IX
Phone: 514.327.4554
Hours: Mon-Wed 11:30am-10pm; until 11pm Thur-Sun
Credit cards: V, MC, Interac; Alcohol: all
Wheelchair access: entrance yes; restroom no
Average main dish: $10 (Prices include taxes)

Le Tropico is a Haitian hot spot way up north on Pie-IX.

Grillot (or griot) is a signature Haitian dish and they do a spicy and tasty version with boneless cubes of grilled marinated pork. The patties have a flaky pastry and savoury chicken filling. Most dishes can be ordered fried or in sauce. The red snapper is an extra large portion of meltingly tender whole fish in a sumptuous sauce. They have goat, chicken, stew, turkey, and conch. Everything is prepared well, respecting the basic qualities of the fresh ingredients, and not masking the food with a long list of extra ingredients. Hot sauce on the side has a mellow heat. Dishes are served with traditional rice and beans, twice-fried plantains, and a small green salad. Tropical juices add a perfect touch. This is authentic Haitian cooking, with all the tastes of Créole cuisine. Everywhere you find lime juice, sour orange, and hot peppers among the layers of flavour.

The Charles family opened Le Tropico in 1998 and they run the kitchen with a sure and steady hand. They serve authentic Haitian home cooking—they don't take flights of fancy into new territory. The décor is basic but it's comfortable with tablecloths, bistro chairs, plants, mango-coloured curtains, and lots of light coming through the windows. It's mostly non-smoking. There are special deals Monday to Wednesday: buy one and get the second at half price. On Sunday children under 12 eat free if accompanied by an adult. Take-out is a large part of their business, and they cater too. This is Créole home cooking up north!

Villa Wellington

4701 Wellington (Verdun at 2nd Ave.)
Métro: De l'Eglise
Phone: 514.768.0102
Hours: Tue-Sun 11am-11pm; closed Monday
Credit cards: V, MC, Amex, Interac; Alcohol: all
Wheelchair access: yes
Seafood platter for two: $17

It's worth the trip to Verdun for this Peruvian restaurant.

Potatoes are native to Peru and Peruvians are very partial to them. The menu includes many different kinds of potatoes—all deliciously prepared. The daily soup is a substantial dish and a good buy. Daily specials include an appetizer and a main dish with vegetables. Starters include a stuffed potato, soft and fragrant tamales, and boiled potatoes with a cheese sauce. Main dishes for the specials include marinated chicken, beef stew with coriander, and fried pork. There are also many à la carte dishes such as ceviche, seafood soup, grilled fish, delicious fried squid, and grilled trout. Peru has a long coastline on the South Pacific Ocean and seafood is an important part of the cuisine. The heaping fried seafood plate (enough for two) is so wonderful it defies description! There is also a choice of non-Peruvian dishes, basic Italian and Greek food, but it's best to ignore them and go for the Peruvian specialties they do well and you can't get elsewhere. Forget the desserts, you won't have room anyway, platters are full to overflowing!

The décor is Peruvian, with hand-woven tablecloths under plastic, and paper placemats—nothing fancy. This is a neighbourhood family restaurant and although the staff is Latin, the clientèle is mixed. Latin music adds to the good feeling about the place. Owner August Saravia is a Peruvian who now lives in Verdun and he opened the restaurant in 1992, offering no-frills food at bargain basement prices. Corona beer goes very well with the Peruvian specialties. You'll enjoy the food here, especially the seafood and the potatoes!

Village Mon Nan

1098 Clark St. (near René-Lévesque)
Métro: St-Laurent or Place d'Armes
Phone: 514.879.9680
Hours: Sun-Mon & Wed-Thur 11am-11pm;
    until midnight Fri & Sat; closed Tuesday
Credit cards: V, MC, Amex; Alcohol: all
Wheelchair access: no
Peking Duck (for three): $27

Village Mon Nan in Chinatown specializes in exquisite Peking duck available at all times, without pre-ordering.

The menu contains a whole range of Peking and Shanghai style dishes, and the kitchen does them well, but the Peking duck is so tempting that it's hard to order anything else. The duck is served in three delicious courses. The first course is duck sliced thin with crispy skin intact, ready to be rolled up in small paper-thin warm pancakes with scallions and hoisin sauce. That taste is unforgettable! The second course is a duck and vegetable stir-fry. Be sure you get the finale, duck soup with thin clear noodles. The duck dinner feeds three comfortably. You might want to order steamed rice to go with it. If you are four, you can stretch it by starting with their delicious steamed or fried dumplings, or whatever strikes your fancy from the menu. You could also order two ducks, but you'll probably need a doggie bag as well.

This is a pleasant resto upstairs from the Mon Nan, which serves Cantonese food. John Lee manages both. Peking duck master chef Chef Yip, who moved from the old Shantung restaurant to the Village Mon Nan, does it all. Service can sometimes be a little offhand. When a craving for Peking duck hits, this is the place to go!

The Sex of Restaurants

Josh Freed

There is no task more daunting to the average anglo than making a restaurant reservation—the ultimate cultural survival test.

In Ontario, any fool can make a reservation—you must open the phone book and look up your restaurant. But in Quebec, you must first know the *sex* of your restaurant.

Let's say you want a reservation at a little place you heard about from some friends—the Viaduc restaurant.

But is it masculine: le Viaduc? Or feminine: la Viaduc? Or could it be listed under something tricky—like Le Restaurant La Viaduc?

It's not easy to remember your genders when you're standing in a phone booth, in −34°, with your gloves off. And even when you consult your pocket dictionary and find that Viaduc is masculine, your search has just begun.

Is it Restaurant Le Viaduc, or Restaurant du Viaduc? Restaurant les Viaducs, or Restaurant des Viaducs? All are grammatically correct.

It could also be listed under Restaurant Chez Viaduc or Restaurant Chez le Viaduc (over 100 restaurants are listed under Chez alone.) Not to mention Restaurant au Viaduc, Restaurant aux Viaducs or Le Restaurant aux Viaducs.

Get one pronoun wrong and you eat at home.

And who's to say the Viaduc is actually classified as a restaurant? It might be listed as a café, and if so, is it a café-restaurant or a restaurant-café?

Or could it be something trendy, like a café-terrace? Each of these have separate listings—hundreds of pages apart.

You don't believe me? Check the Montreal phone book. There are listings for restaurant-bars and bar-restaurants. For restaurant-bistros and bistro-cafés, There are restaurant-charcuteries, restaurant-patisseries, restaurant-pizzerias, and restaurant-brochetteries.

Not to mention brochetterie-restaurants.

It's not easy being an anglophone on the telephone. Or afterwards. Because once you've found your restaurant and showed up for your reservation, you still have to order.

Hmmm—now what's the sex of Caesar salad?

From *Fear of Frying and Other Fax of Life* by Josh Freed. Winner of the Stephen Leacock Prize for Humour. Published by Véhicule Press.

Cheap Thrills *Classics*

Restaurants which have appeared in previous editions. Due to the quality of the food and/or unique dining experience, they are the epitome of a "Cheap Thrill."

Agostini 17
Bangkok 20
Batory Euro-Deli 22
Belles Soeurs, Les 24
Binerie Mont-Royal, La 25
Café International 31
Café Presto 33
Carreta, La 35
Chalet Bar B-Q 37
Chilenita, La 40
Délices de l'Ile Maurice, Les 45
Govinda Jaya Jaya 53
Grand Comptoir, Le 54
Hwang-Kum House 57
Jardin de Jade Poon Kai 60
Kamela Couscous 62
Kei Phat 61
Keur Fatou 63
Ma's Place 65
Maison du Bedouin, La 67
Malhi Sweets 68
Mavi 70
Mazurka 71
Petit Alep, Le 78
Pizza Cachère Pita 81
Première Moisson 82
Puca Puca 83
Pushap 84
Quartier Perse 85
Rotisserie Panama 90

Specialty Index

Kosher
Pizza Cachère Pita 81

Lebanese
Shish-Kebab 97

Mauritian
Délices de l'Ile Maurice,
 Les 45

Mexican
Hacienda, La 55

Moroccan
Maison du Bedouin, La 67

North African
Kamela Couscous 62
Maison du Bedouin, La 67
Nomad, Le 74

Peruvian
Puca Puca 83
Villa Wellington 103

Polish
Batory Euro-Deli 22
Chopin 41
Mazurka 71

Portuguese
Mavi 70
Roi du Plateau 87

Pub
McKibbin's Irish Pub 72

Québécois
Belles Soeurs, Les 24

Binerie Mont-Royal, La 25
Chez Clo 39

Russian
Georgia 52

Salvadoran
Carreta, La 35
El Rincón 48

Senegalese
Keur Fatou 63

Sri Lankan
Jaarl Paadi 58

Syrian/Armenian
Petit Alep, Le 78

Thai
Bangkok 20
Chuch 42
Echalote Restaurant 47
Kei Phat 61
Phad Thai 79

Tunisian
Kamela Couscous 62

Ukrainian
Georgia 52

Vegetarian
Chuch 42
Govinda Jaya Jaya 53
Pizza Cachère Pita 81
Pushap 84

Vietnamese
Echalote Restaurant 47
Hoai Huong 56
Pho Bang New York 80

West African
Abidjanaise, L' 15
Congo-Léo 44
Keur Fatou 63

Neighbourhood Index

Villeray
El Rincón 48

Ville St-Laurent
Diogènes 46
Ma's Place 65

Westmount
Tao 101

Send us Your Suggestions

We are always interested in finding out about new
restaurants for the next edition of
Cheap Thrills Montreal.

Visit us on the Web:

www.vehiculepress.com

www.cheapthrillsguides.com

Véhicule Press